Praise for *The Jewish Odyssey of George Eliot*

"In this compelling and inspiring narrative, elegantly woven from strands historical, biographical, philosophical, and literary, our finest historian of Victorian England provides a brilliant interpretation of *Daniel Deronda*, the final novel of Victorian England's greatest novelist, vindicating its artistic integrity and intellectual importance against its many critics. Ms. Himmelfarb also illuminates George Eliot's remarkably prescient and still relevant perspectives on Zionism and 'the Jewish Question,' concluding with her own profound reflections on the intimate connections of religion and politics to personal identity. A *tour de force*."

> —Leon R. Kass and Amy A. Kass, The University of Chicago

"Miss Himmelfarb, in characteristically diamond-cutting prose, takes up the riddle of Eliot's special interest in Jewish renewal and nationhood long before Zionism even had a name. *The Jewish Odyssey of George Eliot* is a masterful and many-faceted account of Eliot's influences, sources, historical surroundings, changing views and latter-day defense of Judaism."

> —Caitrin Nicol, *The Washington Times*

"In *The Jewish Odyssey of George Eliot*, a brave and bravura excavation of a prophetic artist's mind, Gertrude Himmelfarb at last opens to us the George Eliot who has too long been snubbed—sometimes on aesthetic grounds, but more often with full disparaging intent. In so doing, Himmelfarb catapults George Eliot into the thick of the great central maelstrom of our own moment, when *Daniel Deronda* ceases to be a Victorian novel only, and boldly enters the twenty-first century. Through the lenses of history, culture, philosophy, politics, and literary art, Himmelfarb, in this innovative and dazzling study, reveals how *Daniel Deronda*—not unlike *Uncle Tom's Cabin*—has had its role in succoring and renewing a people; and how it serves as a prescient rebuke to both Sartre and Said."

> —Cynthia Ozick

"Gertrude Himmelfarb leads us through the mystery of why, in the 1870s, Britain's leading novelist, a woman with no Jewish connections, should have chosen to write a book about Jewish identity and the return to Zion. A masterly work, sensitive, profoundly moving, and exceptionally timely."

> —Sir Jonathan Sacks, Chief Rabbi of the United
> Hebrew Congregations of the Commonwealth

Praise for *The People of the Book*

"Gertrude Himmelfarb has brought her unrivalled knowledge, penetrating intellect, and elegant wit to the examination of the phenomenon of philosemitism, and in so doing identifies those brave but all too few Britons who have supported the Jews. Not coincidentally, they have tended to include, from Oliver Cromwell to Winston Churchill, many of the very greatest of the British Gentiles over the past three and a half centuries."

—Andrew Roberts, author of *Storm of War*

"England has a long history of philosemitism and Gertrude Himmelfarb recounts it with insight and understanding. This is an important book, which will encourage those who believe that the safety of the Jewish people and the integrity of Israel are essential to the preservation of Western civilization."

—Paul Johnson, eminent British historian and author

"In a decade when Britain is increasingly portrayed as antisemitic, Gertrude Himmelfarb shows the strength of British philosemitism over four centuries. She has marshalled an impressive array of contemporary evidence, and uses the dispassionate scrutiny of true scholarship both to illuminate the past and to inspire hope for the future."

—Sir Martin Gilbert, Historian, Churchill biographer

the JEWISH ODYSSEY *of* GEORGE ELIOT

GERTRUDE HIMMELFARB

ENCOUNTER BOOKS ℯ NEW YORK • LONDON

First American edition published in 2009 by Encounter Books, an activity of Encounter for Culture and Education, Inc., a nonprofit, tax exempt corporation. Encounter Books website address: www.encounterbooks.com

Manufactured in the United States and printed on acid-free paper. The paper used in this publication meets the minimum requirements of ANSI/NISO Z39.48-1992 (R1997) (*Permanence of Paper*).

First paperback edition published in 2012.
Paperback edition ISBN: 978-1-59403-596-8

The Library of Congress has cataloged the hardcover edition as follows:

Himmelfarb, Gertrude.
The Jewish odyssey of George Eliot/Gertrude Himmelfarb.
p. cm.
Includes bibliographical references and index.
ISBN-13: 978-1-59403-251-6 (alk. paper)
ISBN-10: 1-59403-251-3 (alk. paper)
1. Eliot, George, 1819–1880. Daniel Deronda. 2. Eliot, George, 1819–1880—Characters—Jews. 3. Eliot, George, 1819-1880—Religion.
4. Zionism in literature. 5. Judaism in literature.
6. Jews in literature. I. Title.
PR4658.H46 2009
823'.8—dc22
2008048671

for

BILL AND SUSAN, LIZ AND CALEB

CONTENTS

PROLOGUE

It is one of the curiosities of English literary history, and of Jewish literary history as well, that the most remarkable English novel about Jews, taking Judaism seriously as a faith and anticipating the idea of a Jewish state, should have been written by a non-Jew—a Victorian woman, moreover, who was generally regarded by her contemporaries, as well as by some later critics, as the greatest English novelist of her time. Yet in biographical and critical studies of George Eliot, *Daniel Deronda* is often dismissed as something of an anomaly, an inexplicable and somewhat unfortunate turn in her life and work.

Eliot herself suspected (rightly, as it turned out) that "the Jewish element" in it was likely to "satisfy nobody."[1] Many critics, at the time and since, have found that "element"—the discovery by Deronda of his Jewish identity and with it a Jewish mission—an intrusion in what would otherwise have been a great novel, perhaps her greatest novel. Almost three-quarters of a century later, the eminent literary critic F. R. Leavis gave *Daniel Deronda* a coveted place in the "Great

Tradition" of the novel, suggesting that this deformity, as he saw it, could easily have been excised from it. Years later he did just that, preparing an edition of the novel shorn of the Jewish element, under the title *Gwendolen Harleth*. (That book never appeared only because his publisher had second thoughts about it.)[2]

Eliot would have been appalled by such an emasculation. "I meant everything in the book," she insisted, "to be related to everything else there."[3] If the novel itself was all of a whole, there remains the question of whether it was also all of a whole with the rest of Eliot's life and work. "September, 1856," she wrote in a memorandum of that date, "made a new era in my life, for it was then that I began to write fiction."[4] It was also then that she ceased to be the Mary Anne Evans of her birth-name, or the anonymous contributor to the *Westminster Review*, or the "Marian Evans" whose name appeared as the translator of Feuerbach's *The Essence of Christianity*, and became instead "George Eliot," the author of *Amos Barton,* her first work of fiction which appeared the following year.[*] The novelist, however, was not as sharply demarcated from the essayist or translator as the change of name might suggest. The last and most challenging of her novels, *Daniel Deronda,* was, in a sense, a retrospect of her life and mind, a refashioning of the moral, social, and religious themes that had always occupied her, in one form or another.

---

* Née Mary Anne Evans, she altered her given names, first to Mary Ann, then to Marianne, and finally to Marian. "George" is presumed to have come from George Lewes, with whom she was then living. She herself explained that she took a masculine name to make sure that the book would be taken seriously. In fact, there were many serious and successful female novelists in Victorian England who retained their own names.

Daniel Deronda was not a *jeu d'esprit*—a "Jew d'esprit," as was said mockingly of Disraeli's Jewish novels. Published in 1876, it was a meticulously planned and executed work, very much a product of the mature George Eliot. And lest the book be dismissed, as Disraeli's novels were, as a mere novel, a romance or fantasy, Eliot returned to the theme two years later in an essay that was a passionate defense of Judaism and a Jewish state. Written while she was attending to George Lewes (her husband in all but name) on his deathbed, the essay appeared soon after his death. It was the last chapter of her last book. Eliot herself died two years later.

If biographers have not taken seriously the "Jewish element" in *Daniel Deronda*, or in George Eliot herself, it is perhaps because there have been other anomalies in her life and work to intrigue them. There was, most notably, her relationship with Lewes, a married man, the father of four children, who could not get divorced because he lacked the legal grounds for it, having condoned his wife's affair with his good friend, Thornton Hunt, who was himself married and with whom Lewes's wife had four more children. (Twice Hunt had children with his wife and Mrs. Lewes within weeks of each other.) Earlier, Eliot was suspected, by both his wife and his mistress, of contemplating an affair with John Chapman, the publisher of the *Westminster Review* which she was editing and in whose house she was living. This would have amounted to a *ménage à quatre*. (Eliot did not know that the governess in the household was also Chapman's mistress.) And before that she had been rumored as engaged to the philosopher Herbert Spencer, who described them as "on very intimate terms" (using "intimate" in the Victorian sense that did not necessarily imply sexual intimacy). They both denied those rumors, insisting that they were simply good friends.[5]*

It was a rather free and easy circle in which Eliot moved in these years. And while there was nothing free and easy in the domestic life of Lewes and Eliot—theirs was a proper and entirely monogamous marriage, in all but name—the fact that they lived together openly, not secretively, was provocative enough in Victorian England. And it was still more provocative in the case of Eliot, the premier moralist of that very moralistic age, who blatantly defied one of its basic principles, the sanctity of marriage. Yet her reputation (literary as well as moral) was such that it surmounted this impropriety. If she was ostracized by a few, she was lionized by many others, including nobility and even royalty. She had more dinner invitations than she cared to accept, and people were honored to be asked to her regular Saturday evening or Sunday afternoon "at homes."

Latter-day feminists, who find this aspect of Eliot appealing, are put off by the fact that she herself tried to put a conventional gloss on this unconventional relationship, insisting on being addressed as Mrs. Lewes, to which the real Mrs. Lewes, among others, obligingly acquiesced. (She signed her personal letters "Marian Lewes" or "M. E. Lewes.") After Lewes died, she married (rather hastily and briefly—she died within the year) a much younger man, John Cross, with all the trappings of a proper marriage: a trousseau, a church wedding, and a honeymoon. (Her friends were more shocked by this mar-

---

* They remained good friends. Years later, at a committee meeting of the London Library, Edmund Gosse recalled Spencer's strong objection to the purchase of novels for the library, "except, of course," Spencer insisted, "those of George Eliot."[6]

riage than they had been by her non-marriage with Lewes.) A more serious affront to feminists, at the time and since, was her refusal to support John Stuart Mill's amendment to the suffrage bill of 1867, which would have given women the vote. They could hardly be reassured by her explanation that just because the woman has "the worse share in existence," that was all the more reason for "a sublimer resignation in woman and a more regenerating tenderness in man."[7]

Yet feminists might have found a powerful advocate for their cause in one of the most fascinating characters in *Daniel Deronda*, Deronda's mother. Compared with her passionate plea for liberation—a liberation from the conventional role assigned to women by Judaism even more than by bourgeois society—Mill's speech on the suffrage and his essay on "The Subjection of Women" were academic and anemic. The mother's account of her artistic aspirations and achievements, the compromises and sacrifices she had to make for her career (giving up her son, most notably), made her rendition of the feminist argument all the more compelling. By the same token, it made Deronda's rejection of that argument all the more interesting. The Judaism his mother found so restrictive (for men as well as women), he found liberating, providing women (as well as men) a dignity and a humanity that transcended the freedom and equality sought so desperately by his mother.

The mother's tale is still more intriguing, for it suggests affinities with Eliot herself, who was no less strong-minded and strong-willed, who defied her father and teachers, embraced ideas that were radical and heretical, and flouted the sexual (or at least marital) conventions of her society. Yet she no less firmly rejected, as Deronda did, the kind of liberation his mother argued for so passionately. So far from giving up her son to be raised by another, Eliot, though she had no children of her own, was very much involved with Lewes's children, quite as if she was their mother. Deronda's mother might be a model for a latter-day feminist. Eliot quite definitely was not.

Daniel Deronda raises another issue that may seem even more anomalous, and more seriously so. Eliot is generally represented not only as a great moralist but also as a firm "unbeliever," as the Victorians delicately put it.[8] This is what so impressed her contemporary, the noted historian Lord Acton. A Catholic tormented by what he saw as the moral flaws in the history of Christianity, he praised Eliot as a great moral teacher, "a consummate expert in the pathology of conscience." In an age "distracted between the intense need of believing and the difficulty of belief," Eliot managed to "reconcile the practical ethics of unbelief and of belief," making of atheism a worthy moral rival of Christianity.[9] Nietzsche testified to the same quality in Eliot, although in a less complimentary manner, when he decried those "little moralistic females à la Eliot" who became "moral fanatics" to compensate for their religious emancipation. "They are rid of the Christian God and now believe all the more firmly that they must cling to Christian morality."[10]

Why then, having got "rid of the Christian God," did Eliot take so kindly to the Jewish God embraced by Deronda—a moral God, to be sure, as Deronda understood Him, but also a religious God, presiding over a people who revered a holy Scripture, observed ancient laws and rituals, and regarded themselves as the chosen people? Eliot's own religious odyssey had taken her from the conventional low-church Anglicanism of her family, to the rigorous Evangelicalism of her youth, and finally to the agnosticism or, as some thought it, the atheism of her mature years. Her "unbelief," moreover, derived not from the humanistic positivism of Auguste Comte, then popular in England (whom Lewes had written about), but from the more aggressive assault upon religion in general, and Christianity and Judaism in particular, by such heretics, renowned on the continent, as David Strauss, Ludwig Feuerbach, and Spinoza, whom Eliot had not only read but translated. Why, having gone so far in the rejection of religion, did she then make a hero of Daniel Deronda, who championed Judaism not merely as a venerable relic of antiquity, nor even as the begetter of Christianity, but as a living, vibrant religion, a religion, moreover, that contained within itself the promise of nationhood and statehood?

Her contemporaries did not know quite what to make of this. One reviewer of *Daniel Deronda* praised it for emanating "so distinctly religious a tone. . . . [T]he story is essentially religious."[11] Two years later, another reviewer of her volume of essays described her as "the first great godless writer of fiction that has appeared in England, . . . the first legitimate fruit of our modern atheistic pietism."[12] Was Eliot of two minds about religion—or perhaps only about Judaism, which would be even more curious? How did the translator of Strauss, Feuerbach, and Spinoza come to write so sympathetic a novel about Judaism and so prophetic a vision of Zionism?

For that matter, what inspired Eliot (whose formal schooling stopped at the age of sixteen) to undertake the formidable amount of research into the literature, history, creeds, and practices of Judaism—research that went well beyond the needs of the novel itself? Her notebooks comprise hundreds of pages of excerpts from the Bible and prophets, the Talmud and medieval commentators, modern German scholars of the *Wissenschaft des Judentums* movement (the scientific study of Judaism), and a multitude of other works in Latin, Greek, German, French, and, of course, English. She also took lessons in Hebrew, for which purpose she acquired Hebrew dictionaries, lexicons, and grammars. In the published volume of her notebooks, the list of books she consulted comprise twenty-three pages.[13]

For the most part, Eliot bore her learning lightly. It would take an erudite scholar to identify the source of some of the allusions in the novel or the significance of the names of some of the characters.[14] Even at her most pedantic, she did not fully reveal the extent of her knowledge. The epigraph to one of the chapters is formidable enough: a quotation in German from a work by one of the founders of the *Wissenschaft des Judentums* school, Leopold Zunz. Translated into English, it also appears as the opening paragraph of that chapter:

> If there are ranks in suffering, Israel takes precedence of all the nations—if the duration of sorrows and patience with which they are borne ennoble, the Jews are among the aristocracy of every land—if a literature is called rich in the possession of a few classic tragedies, what shall we say to a National Tragedy lasting for fifteen hundred years, in which the poets and the actors were also the heroes?

Deronda, Eliot explained, "had lately been reading that passage."[15] He could have read it (although we are not told this) in an English translation included in a recently published volume of Hebrew literature. But Eliot herself had read it in the original, in Leopold Zunz's *Die Synagogale Poesie des Mittelalters*, and it is her translation of this passage that appears in the novel.[16]

Why, finally, did Eliot choose to write this book at this time, when the "Jewish question" was of no great public concern, certainly not in England? A literary critic might be tempted to think of Daniel Deronda as a foil to that other notable fictional Jew, Dickens's Fagin—two actors in a morality play, with Deronda, the arch-hero triumphing over Fagin, the arch-villain. But there is no suggestion that Eliot had Fagin or any other literary stereotypes of Jews in mind when she wrote her novel. Nor were there any public events to provoke her—nothing like a Damascus Affair (the prosecution of Jews in Syria in 1840 on the charge of ritual murder), or a Dreyfus Affair (the accusation of treason in 1894 against a Jewish officer in France), or the pogroms in Russia in 1881 which sent a surge of Jews, poor and conspicuously foreign, into England, arousing the hostility of many Englishmen and the sympathy of a few. (Had Eliot's novel been written a few years later, it would surely have been attributed to the shocking news of the pogroms.) There was not even the political issue of Jewish citizenship to focus attention upon Jews; that had been settled long before with the Jewish emancipation bill of 1858.

There was, in fact, no serious "Jewish question"—in England, at any rate—to stimulate Eliot's imagination or inspire her to write about Jews and Judaism as she did. She did not have to create likeable characters to compensate for unlikeable stereotypes, or promote a cause like Zionism as a response to persecution and anti-Semitism.* Even the familiar kind of anti-Jewish prejudices played little part in *Daniel Deronda*. They were noted in passing and were of the mildest order. Certainly they did not explain the evolving character of Deronda as he discovered his Jewish lineage. There might have been drama enough in the struggle of an enlightened, liberal Jew seeking to take his rightful place in a less than enlightened and liberal England. But that was not the drama Eliot had in mind for her hero. Instead she had Deronda choose a very different kind of Jewish identity and mission.

Eliot has been credited by historians and eulogized by Jews as the prophetic inspirer of Zionism and of the state of Israel. There is some warrant for those claims. *Daniel Deronda* appeared twenty-one years before the first meeting of the Zionist Congress in Basle and seventy-two years before the establishment of the state of Israel. But Eliot was a Zionist with a difference. When Deronda emigrated to Palestine, he did so not out of the fear of pogroms, or as a response to a Holocaust, or even to escape the barbs and slights of the English mode of polite anti-Semitism, but rather to fulfill a proud and unique heritage. His mentor, Mordecai, was a learned as well as a passionate Jew who felt in his soul, as he said, the faith and the history of his people—his "nation." It was this

---

* Both "anti-Semitism" and "Zionism" were later terms of foreign origin. "Anti-Semitism" first appeared in 1879 in a book by Wilhelm Marr, *Der Weg zum Siege des Germantums über des Judentums* (*The Way to Victory over Judaism*), as a prelude to his founding of the *Antisemiten-Lage* (League of Antisemites). "Zionism" was coined in 1890 by an Austrian Jew, Nathan Birnbaum, who founded a nationalist Jewish student movement and played a prominent part, with Theodor Herzl, in the first Zionist Congress in Basle in 1897. (Birnbaum also had the distinction, after turning against political Zionism, of becoming the first Secretary General of the pro-religious and anti-Zionist organization, Agudath Israel.)

sense of nationality that inspired his vision of Judaism and that he transmitted to his disciple Deronda. And it was this theme that Eliot returned to in her last essay, when she likened Jewish nationality to the admirable sentiment that had inspired her own countrymen in their evolution as a nation.

If Eliot has become a heroine to later generations of Zionists, she has also become the villain for the postcolonial school that sees Zionism as the expression of the "hegemonic imperialism" that has oppressed the original and rightful natives of Palestine, indeed denying or ignoring their very existence. Edward Said took *Daniel Deronda* as the prime example of this nefarious ideology in *The Question of Palestine*, in 1979 (a sequel to his influential book, *Orientalism*). It has since become a staple of some literary critics, who have gone on to make Eliot personally, as well as ideologically, complicitous with imperialism by investing in colonial enterprises.

Important books have an afterlife for which their authors may have little responsibility. That afterlife, however remote from the original, testifies to the enduring vitality of the book itself. One returns to *Daniel Deronda* not only to correct the record, so to speak, but also to engage anew with a novel that is truly in the "great tradition" of the novel—and to return, by way of the novel, to its equally memorable author.

Daniel Deronda was as much an act of self-discovery for Eliot as it was for Deronda, an intellectual and spiritual odyssey into the foreign world of Judaism. In the course of that odyssey, Eliot encountered "the Jewish question," as it was known on the continent, the question of the proper role of Jews in a Christian society, or, as others preferred, in a secular society. It was this question that hovered behind "the Jewish element" in the novel, which some critics thought distracting or extraneous, but which, as Eliot insisted, was at its very heart. Eliot's understanding of the Jewish question, and thus her response to it, was very different from that of most of her contemporaries. This is what made her novel so provocative at the time. And it is what continues to make it so pertinent and challenging today.

I.

"THE JEWISH QUESTION"

Daniel Deronda was the only one of Eliot's novels to be set in the present. But it has a rich background in history, as well as in Eliot's personal life. Eliot was not only cognizant of that history—the history of the Jewish question as it emerged on the continent and, in a different form, in England—she herself was involved in some of its critical episodes. It was an essential element in her Jewish odyssey, as it was in the novel itself.

As a practical, public issue, the Jewish question, in the late eighteenth and nineteenth centuries, was the question of citizenship. It was in this sense that France is credited with having solved that question in 1791 when it enfranchised the Jews. But it did so in the same equivocal spirit that the Enlightenment had brought to the subject. The *philosophes*, in principle committed to the idea of religious liberty, were also committed to an idea of reason so antithetical to religion as to deprive religious creeds of credibility and religious institutions of moral legitimacy.

L'infâme, in Voltaire's "*Ecrasez l'infâme,*" was Christianity and, more particularly, the Catholic Church. But Judaism, the progenitor of Christianity, was even more infamous, as were the Jews themselves, "an ignorant and barbarous people," Voltaire wrote in his *Philosophical Dictionary*, "who have long united the most sordid avarice with the most detestable superstition and the most invincible hatred for every people by whom they are tolerated and enriched." "Still," Voltaire generously conceded, "we ought not to burn them."[1] On other occasions, his remarks were more ominous. "You [Jews] have surpassed all nations in impertinent fables, in bad conduct, and in barbarism. You deserve to be punished, for this is your destiny."[2]* Jews did not fare much better in the hands of Diderot, the co-editor of the *Encyclopédie* and the prototype of the *philosophe*, who criticized the Jews for their obscurity, fanaticism, and blind respect for authority—"in a word, all the defects indicative of an ignorant and supersititious nation"; or d'Holbach, who carried rationalism to its ultimate form of materialism and devoted an entire book to an attack upon the "stupid Hebrews" as the source of all fanaticism and persecution.[4]

Rousseau and Montesquieu were more sympathetic to Jews and Judaism, perhaps because they were less committed to the ideal of reason and less hostile to religion. Rousseau favored a civil religion as a necessary part of the social con-

---

* Voltaire's "vituperation" against Jews (as Eliot once put it) was well known at the time. Since then, admirers of Voltaire have tried to minimize his diatribes by ignoring or paraphrasing rather than quoting them, and have explained them away by suggesting that the real culprit was Christianity and that it was only because of the censor that Voltaire had to use the Jews as a surrogate villain.[3]

tract, and Montesquieu approved of an established church on the model of England. Rousseau referred to Jews only in passing, in *Emile*, for example, when he deplored the fact that Jews were not free to speak out so that others had no way of judging them rightly, and in his book on the government of Poland, where Moses appeared as one of the three great "legislators" of antiquity.* Montesquieu was more effusive in his admiration of Jews, praising them for their contributions to commerce (atttibuting to them, for example, the invention of letters of exchange), and more eloquently in a long "Remonstrance to the Inquisitors of Spain and Portugal," ostensibly written by a Jew protesting against the burning of a young Jewess at an *auto-da-fé* in Lisbon.[6]

As the heir of the Enlightenment, the Revolution inherited its principles and its ambiguities. The first article of the Declaration of the Rights of Man and the Citizen, proclaimed in August 1789, pronounced all men "free and equal in rights," and the sixth declared "all citizens, being equal in the eyes of the law, . . . equally eligible to all dignities and to all public positions and occupations." On the face of it, Jews seemed to be emancipated and enfranchised. The catch came in the word "citizens." Shortly after the Declaration,

---

* Eliot had read *Emile* and the *Social Contract*, but it was the *Confessions* that had a riveting effect upon her. When she met Emerson in 1848, he asked her what had "awakened her to deep reflection." Her answer was Rousseau's *Confessions*. (Carlyle, Emerson told her, had given the same answer.) To a friend several months later, she said that even if Rousseau's views were grievously wrong, "the fire of his genius" sent an "electric thrill through my intellectual and moral frame."[5] She and Lewes read aloud the *Confessions*, *Emile*, and *Julie, ou la nouvelle Héloïse* when they were abroad in the summer of 1876, at the same time that *Daniel Deronda* was appearing serially in England.

the Assembly passed decrees distinguishing between active and passive citizens, only the former having the right to vote and bear arms. In addition to such obvious criteria as age, place of residence, and payment of taxes, the active citizen also had "to be or have become French." The last clause had special pertinence to Jews, for it raised the question of whether all Jews, or only some Jews, were or had become "French," and thus could qualify as active citizens. In January 1790, a tumultuous debate on the subject was closed by Mirabeau, who declared the Jew a citizen only if he was more *un homme*, a man, than a Jew. A Jew who was more a Jew than an *homme* could not be a citizen; indeed, anyone who did not want to become an *homme* should be banished from the new society being created by the revolution. The Assembly concluded, by a vote of 374 to 280, to grant the rights of active citizenship to Sephardi Jews, some three or four thousand of them specified as "Portuguese, Spanish and Avignonnais Jews."

When the issue was raised again a year later, the question focussed upon the much larger number of Ashkenazi Jews, settled mainly in Alsace-Lorraine, who seemed more Jew than *homme*. More religious than the Sephardi, less assimilated, and very much a community, the Ashkenazi were charged with being a "nation within a nation." After a long debate, these thirty thousand Jews were declared citizens—as individuals, however, not as members of a religious community. Count Clermont-Tonnerre, the deputy from Paris and the chief supporter of the motion, put the case most clearly. Those Jews who wanted to be citizens had to "disavow their judges" and eliminate their "Jewish corporations." "Jews, as individuals," he announced, "deserve everything; Jews as a nation nothing. . . . There can only be the individual citizen."[7]

After the restoration of the monarchy, French Jews were warmly received by one group of radicals and vilified by another. The technocratic socialists inspired by Saint-Simon, looking to scientists, industrialists, and financiers to bring about a productive economy and an egalitarian society, found ready disciples among Jewish (and converts from Judaism) industrialists, bankers, and intellectuals. Among the more prominent Saint-Simonians were the Péreire brothers, Jewish bankers and entrepreneurs who competed with the Rothschilds for the domination of the French banking system. When the Saint-Simonian movement, in 1830, took on a revivalist, messianic character, a search was initiated for a new messiah, a Jewess from the Orient, who would be the "Mother" of the new moral and social order. The presence of so many well-established Jews in the movement, as well as its philo-Semitic ideology, brought out the not so latent anti-Semitism of other socialists, who denounced it as a Jewish plot to subvert civilization.

The socialists Fourier and Proudhon did not need Saint-Simonianism to provoke them; they were anti-Semitic on other grounds. Charles Fourier declared the granting of citizenship to Jews one of the most shameful of all of society's recent "vices." "The Jews, with their commercial morality, are they not the leprosy and perdition of the body politic?" Recognizing no fatherland, they were even more parasitical than the other merchants among whom they lived. Instead of liberating them as citizens, Fourier wrote, the government should constrain them in every way, and ultimately, by one means or another, remove them from France. Pierre-Joseph Proudhon, the socialist *cum* anarchist, was even more vehement. Famous for his dictum "Property is theft," he convicted Jews not only of being consummate capitalists and thus thieves, but also of being an "unsociable, obstinate, infernal race." His solution was simple: "The Jew is the enemy of humankind. The race must either be sent back to Asia or exterminated."[8]*

French Jews were legally enfranchised, but were subjected to repeated denunciations and attacks, sometimes culminating in violence. When the Damascus Affair erupted in 1840, the French consul in Syria publicly and aggressively endorsed the charge of ritual murder, denounced the efforts of the British consul to help the Jews, and advised the French government to "impose a salutary terror upon the Jews."[9] The French government did not take that advice, but did support the charges brought by the Syrians even after they had been exposed as lies, and the French public and press continued to circulate them. Although Jews continued to make advances economically and socially, the undercurrent of hostility was unabated, breaking out in riots in Alsace in 1848. Conditions in the Second Empire were somewhat better, but degenerated with the establishment of the Third Republic in 1870. The revival of anti-Semitism from both the clerical and royalist Right and the socialist followers of Fourier and Proudhon on the Left culminated in the Dreyfus Affair in 1894.

The Jewish question as it evolved in Germany differed philosophically and rhetorically but not substantively from that in France. The German Enlightenment, like the French, was equivocal toward Jews. Kant, for example, was not obsessed

---

* There are several references by Eliot to the Saint-Simonians (in her essay on Heine, for example, in 1856) and to four articles on Proudhon by the literary critic Sainte-Beuve in 1866.

with Jews, as Voltaire was. He said little about them, but what he did say was not flattering.

> The Palestinians living among us have, for the most part, earned a not unfounded reputation for being cheaters, because of their spirit of usury since their exile. Certainly, it seems strange to conceive of a *nation* of cheaters; but it is just as odd to think of a nation of merchants, the great majority of whom, bound by an ancient superstition that is recognized by the State they live in, seek no civil dignity and try to make up for this loss by the advantage of duping the people among whom they find refuge, and even one another.[10]

Nor did Kant have any respect for Judaism as a religion. Indeed it was not a religion, he insisted, still less an ethic, but only a "political organization," an "earthly state," consisting of a "collection of mere statutory laws" about mere earthly matters. Only later, inspired by the Greeks, did this "otherwise ignorant people" acquire the concept of virtue that made for a more enlightened Judaism.[11]

Kant's disciple Fichte was far more outspoken in his distaste for Jews. Although he was an ardent admirer of the French Revolution (and of the Jacobin faction of the Revolution), he criticized the decree enfranchising French Jewry and opposed similar measures that were being proposed in Germany. Other groups, he argued—the military, the nobility, and the church—might be tolerated as states within the nation, but the Jews could not be. "A mighty state stretches across almost all the countries of Europe, hostile in intent and engaged in constant strife with everyone else. . . . This is Jewry." For this "state" there was no room in a modern nation. Jews could be allowed "human rights" permitting them to live in the country as aliens, but not civic rights. "The only way to give them citizenship would be to cut off their heads on the same night in order to replace them with those containing no Jewish ideas."[12]

The ferocity of Fichte's rhetoric is all the more startling because German Jewry at the time was on good terms with much of German society and was enjoying an enlightenment of its own, a *Haskalah* (the Hebrew word meaning reason or mind) designed to bring Judaism into modernity. The most celebrated representative of that movement was Moses Mendelssohn, whose influential book *Jerusalem*, in 1783, portrayed a Judaism that was both rational and ethical, with the Mosaic law serving as the practical codification of the moral law.* Inspired by this philosophy, Jewish educational institutions were created to promote secular as well as religious learning, and Jews were encouraged to enter occupations not traditionally Jewish and to participate actively in the Christian society in which they lived. In effect, the *Haskalah* provided the rationale for Jewish citizenship by allowing for a social and civic assimilation on the part of Jews which did not require any repudiation of Judaism or conversion to Christianity.

To a large extent, the movement succeeded, first in producing Jews who made notable contributions to the secular arts and sciences, and then in giving them entrée into an enlightened society that accepted them as they were, as enlightened Jews. Mendelssohn regarded Kant, for example, as a friend—

---

* Eliot owned a copy of this edition of Mendelssohn's *Jerusalem*, and her *Notebooks* contain excerpts from it as well as personal comments on Mendelssohn himself.

or at least, as a cordial rival and disputant. Earlier in their careers, they had both submitted essays for a prize offered by the Royal Academy in Berlin; Mendelssohn won, Kant took second place, and their essays were published together. Thirty years later, Kant took issue with Mendelssohn's account of the relationship of Christianity and Judaism, which was the basis of Mendelssohn's rejection of the conversion of Jews. In any case, Kant graciously concluded, the sacred texts of Judaism would be preserved, because they would continue to "possess value for scholarship even if not for the benefit of religion."[13]*

During the period of the revolutionary wars, most German Jews were granted citizenship in the states where they resided. After the fall of Napoleon, these rights were revoked and anti-Jewish sentiments flourished anew, among intellectuals as well as the populace. In 1819, a series of riots against Jews—the "Hep! Hep!" riots, as they were known, by the slogan used as their rallying cry—broke out throughout Germany and even spread to some neighboring countries, where they found support among all classes of the population. (The first of the riots was instigated by students opposing commercial and civil rights for Jews.)

It was against this background that Hegel, two years later, in *Philosophy of Right*, vigorously defended the enfranchisement of Jews, in effect rebutting the strictures the French revolutionaries had placed upon Jews. Technically, he granted, Jews might be denied civil rights on the ground that they belonged "not merely to a religious sect but to a foreign

---

* In the latter part of the nineteenth century, the Jewish heirs of the Haskalah—Hermann Cohen, most notably—were prominent in the philosophical movement known as Neo-Kantianism.

race." But the "fierce outcry" raised against them ignored the fact that "they are, above all, *men*," and as such "a person with rights." To exclude the Jews from those rights would be "blameable and reproachable," not only because it would confirm them in their isolation, but also because it would violate the very nature of the state as a political institution.[14]

Hegel's spirited defense of Jewish citizenship was all the more noteworthy because it was in dramatic contrast to some of his disciples, who, in liberating themselves from orthodox Christianity, also launched a vigorous attack upon Judaism. David Strauss's *Life of Jesus,* published in 1835, four years after the death of Hegel, established him as one of the leading lights of the left-wing of the Young Hegelians. (It was he who first classified the Young Hegelians as "right" and "left"— and "center" as well.) Although Strauss insisted that his own work was "the alpha and omega of Hegel's work," he also recognized that it was a radical reinterpretation of Hegel. Where Hegel saw the dialectic of reason, or spirit, as incarnate in Christianity, in the person of Jesus and in the stories of the gospel, Strauss interpreted that dialectic as subversive of orthodox Christianity. Jesus, Strauss conceded, was a historic figure, but the Christ of the gospels was a mythological construct derived from Jewish messianism—a messianic idea, moreover, that was realized not in one individual, in Jesus, but in the community, indeed, in humanity. In this mythological Christ, the divine and the human became one. The fatal error of Judaism, which made it inferior not only to Christianity but to polytheism as well, was its emphasis upon the otherness of God. Thus Judaism totally alienated man from spirit, whereas Christianity, however flawed, at least had the virtue of overcoming that alienation by uniting the divine and the human in the person of Jesus.

In only a few years, the Young Hegelians progressed from neo-Hegelianism to what amounted to anti-Hegelianism and from a mythological Christianity to atheism. Ludwig Feuerbach's *Towards a Critique of Hegelian Philosophy*, in 1839, was a critique of Hegelianism, not a mere reinterpretation. And his *Essence of Christianity* two years later was a rejection not of orthodox or even mythological Christianity but of religion itself. Where Strauss had made of man the creator of the myths that passed as Christianity, Feuerbach made of man the creator of God, a God who was nothing more than a projection and invention of man himself. The God of Israel was worse yet—"nothing but the personified selfishness of the Israelite people, to the exclusion of all other nations." This was the "secret of monotheism," which Judaism had invented and perpetuated—an "absolute intolerance" of all other peoples. "Their principle, their God, is the most practical principle in the world, namely, egoism; and moreover egoism in the form of religion."[15]*

Two other Young Hegelians gave the Jewish question a prominence it had not had—and a label as well.† Bruno Bauer's essay, "The Jewish Question" (published as an article in 1842 and a pamphlet the following year), is known

---

* George Eliot, then Mary Ann Evans, translated Strauss's *Life of Jesus* in 1846 and Feuerbach's *Essence of Christianity* in 1854.
† The expression "the Jewish question" first gained currency at this time. The founding document of Zionism, Theodor Herzl's *Judenstaat*, had as its subtitle "An Attempt at a Modern Solution to the Jewish Question." Today, an Internet search of the phrase first produces the name of Marx, and only later that of Hitler, with his "solution" to that "question."

today mainly because it inspired a critique, under the same title, by his one-time pupil Karl Marx. But it was provocative enough on its own, decreeing all religion illusory and pernicious, and Judaism the most degraded form of religion. Protesting against those who defended Jews on the grounds that they had been oppressed and martyred, Bauer insisted that they had brought that condition upon themselves. They had provoked their enemies by their stubborn adherence to "their law, their language, their whole way of life."[16] Defying history and progress, they contributed nothing to the arts and sciences; clinging tenaciously to their own nationality, they were obviously excluded from the nations of Europe. Even while warring against Christianity, they had the audacity to claim citizenship on a par with Christians, asking the Christian state to abandon its religious principles, while holding firmly to their own. The very idea of citizenship in a Christian state was flawed, because religion itself was a denial of citizenship. The Jew could not claim citizenship unless he ceased being a Jew.

This would seem to be a radical enough account of the Jewish question. (Bauer himself noted that his "understanding of Judaism" was harsher than that of other opponents of Jewish emancipation.)[17] But to Karl Marx, it was insufficiently radical (or harsh), because it required only the religious emancipation of Jews, implying that Jews could be politically emancipated if only they freed themselves of their religion. In his own essay, "On the Jewish Question," in 1844, Marx argued that religious emancipation fell short of "human emancipation." So long as Jews continued to occupy their distinctive role in society, they could not be emancipated. Bauer had considered only the "sabbath Jew." The real problem was the "actual, secular Jew," the "everyday Jew."

What is the secular basis of Judaism? *Practical* need, *self-interest.*

What is the worldly cult of the Jew? *Bargaining.*
What is his worldly god? *Money.*

Very well! Emancipation from *bargaining* and *money*, and thus from practical and real Judaism would be the emancipation of our era. . . .

. . . The *social* emancipation of the Jew is the *emancipation of society from Judaism.*[18]*

In his "Theses on Feuerbach" the following year, Marx criticized Feuerbach for much the same reason. Feuerbach's materialism was faulty because it was theoretical and contemplative rather than practical and active. It reduced the religious world to its secular basis, but did not recognize the self-contradictions in that secular world, contradictions that could be removed only by being "revolutionized in practice." The last of Marx's theses is the most famous: "The philosophers have only interpreted the world, in various ways; the point, however, is to change it." But his first thesis was no less memorable: Feuerbach could not grasp the significance of "revolutionary, of practical-critical activity," because he was

---

* In defense of Marx, we are often reminded that this was the "young Marx," whose quarrel was not with Jews or Judaism but with the economic system they represented—with capitalism, in short. But this essay was neither repudiated nor contradicted by the "mature Marx." Moreover, had it been only capitalism that was at issue, Marx might have conceded that the Jewish proletariat at least might have been admitted to citizenship. But it was their Jewishness that stigmatized them, their devotion to a "worldly God" whose essence was "money," "bargaining," "self-interest." Psychoanalysts and biographers have made much of the fact that Marx himself was a converted Jew, having been baptized at a young age by his father. It is also notable that his father was descended from a long line of distinguished rabbis and scholars, and that his mother was also the daughter of a rabbi.

fixed in the "dirty-judaical form of appearance."[19] In modern parlance, that "dirty-judaical form" is known as capitalism.

One of the few German radicals to rally to the cause of the Jews (although belatedly), was another Young Hegelian, a friend of Marx and his collaborator on the *Rheinische Zeitung*. Moses Hess, in his essay "On Capital" (published in 1845 but written earlier—indeed before Marx's own essay), identified Judaism with capitalism and excoriated the Jews as idolators whose primary god Moloch demanded blood sacrifices.* Hess (who, unlike Marx, knew Hebrew) related the Hebrew word "blood" (*dam*) to the word "money" (*damim*), thus tracing the evolution of the blood sacrifice to the money sacrifice (the cult of money). In his more affectionate moments, Marx called Hess "my communist Rabbi"; at the time, Engels said that Hess was the first of the Young Hegelians to become a communist. Later, as Hess deviated from Marxism, propounding a socialism that was more ethical and altruistic than materialistic, he was derided (although not by name) in the appendix to the *Communist Manifesto* as one of the "German or 'True' Socialists," who invoked such fanciful concepts as "the alienation of humanity" in place of the hard realities of the class struggle.

The full extent of Hess's heresy, however, did not emerge until 1862, with the publication of *Rome and Jerusalem*, a

---

* Only recently has it become known that Hess's essay had been written and sent to Marx for publication in 1843, before Marx himself had written his "On the Jewish Question." Marx's essay, containing images and ideas clearly borrowed from Hess (although not acknowledged as such), was published in 1844; Hess's the following year.[20]

short book in the form of twelve letters ostensibly to a woman friend (a real friend, it is now thought), with ten supplementary notes. The first letter opened with a moving personal testament.

> After twenty years of estrangement I have returned to my
> people. Once again I am sharing in its festivals of joy and
> days of sorrow, in its hopes and memories. I am taking part
> in the spiritual and intellectual struggles of our day, both
> within the House of Israel and between our people and the
> gentile world. . . . A sentiment which I believed I had sup-
> pressed beyond recall is alive once again. It is the thought
> of my nationality, which is inseparably connected with my
> ancestral heritage, with the Holy Land and Eternal City, the
> birthplace of the belief in the divine unity of life and of the
> hope for the ultimate brotherhood of all men.[21]

The "Rome" of the title was not the classical Rome but the contemporary Rome that was aspiring to become the capital of an independent nation. And the subtitle, "The Last Nationality Question," in effect subsumed the Jewish question under the nationality question. "The race struggle," Hess announced, "is the primal one, the class struggle secondary."[22] The brotherhood of men, which was the aim of the class struggle, would be achieved by solving the race struggle. And that required the establishment of a Jewish state—a state based upon the Jewish religion, which was itself egalitarian, recognizing no classes and assuming the unity of mankind. All the alternative strategies, Hess said, had failed. Reform, education, emancipation, assimilation, conversion—none of these had overcome the hatred of Jews by Germans, a hatred not so much of their religion as of their race. The Jew could change his name, his religion, and his character; he could even become a citizen. But he would still be, to the gentile, a Jew. Only the existence of a state, "a spiritual nerve center" for the Jewish people, could earn the Jew—even the Jew who did not live in the state—an identity of which he was proud and which would give him the respect of those among whom he lived [23]

Hess's was a lonely voice at the time, and for some time to come. *Rome and Jerusalem* sold all of 160 copies in its first year, and was virtually unknown for the rest of the century.[24*] Hess himself did not entirely give up the class struggle. As a Marxist delegate to the First International in 1868-1869, he opposed the representatives of Proudhon and Bakunin on the grounds that they were disrupting working-class unity. It was at this time, while Hess was debating the socialist question, that Bismarck, as head of the North German Confederation, was addressing the Jewish question. In 1869 he succeeded in passing legislation granting full civic and political emancipation to the Jews. The following year, in a discussion with a prominent anti-Semite, Bismarck defended mixed marriages between Jews and Christians—especially between rich Jews and German barons. "Money must be made to recirculate," he said, "There is no such thing as an evil race."[26]

England's Jewish question, as one might expect, was very different from that of Germany or even France—far less philo-

---

* In 1898, after publishing *Judenstaat*, Theodor Herzl picked up Hess's book and started to read it, putting it aside until 1901 when he came to it again, read it through, and, as he wrote in his diary, was "enraptured and uplifted" by it (although not, he added, by its Hegelian terminology).[25]

sophical and theological, more prosaic, political, and, above all, temperate. It was nothing more than the simple question of citizenship. How could Jews—or, for that matter, Catholics or Dissenters—be fully accredited citizens of a state with an established church?

This question was debated on and off for a century, starting in 1753 with the introduction of a Jewish Naturalization Bill. The bill was a response to the arrival of recent Jewish refugees, mainly from Germany but also from Poland, Holland, Spain, and Portugal. The "Jew Bill," as it was known, was to provide for the naturalization of Jews who had been resident in Great Britain or Ireland for three years, giving them the same status as their native-born children. The key provision of the bill, and the focus of future debates about citizenship, was the clause exempting the applicant from the taking of the Sacrament, the religious oath prescribed by the Church of England. The bill passed the House of Lords without a division, and the House of Commons by a vote of 96 to 55. Only after the bill received the royal assent and became law did the controversy spill out into the public arena, with anti-Jewish demonstrators making the familiar charges of ritual murders, conspiracies, Jewish gold, and the like. After six months, the act was repealed, first by the House of Lords which made it clear that it did so not for reasons of principle but only in response to the popular clamor, and then, in a more populist spirit, by the House of Commons. The public agitation died down immediately; at its worst there had been no physical violence. (The demonstrations may not have been entirely spontaneous; they coincided with the parliamentary elections and the Tories' attempts to discredit the administration.)

It was the "people out of doors," not political leaders or writers, who fanned the anti-Jewish sentiments that defeated the bill. The major figures in the British Enlightenment, unlike the French, were for the most part well disposed to Jews, or at least not ill disposed to them. Burke's passing references, in the *Reflections on the Revolution in France*, to "money-jobbers, usurers, and Jews" are often quoted as evidence of the familiar stereotypes, as is his description of Lord George Gordon, a convert to Judaism, "heir to the old hoards of the synagogue." But Gordon had earned Burke's enmity because of his leadership in the anti-Catholic riots of 1780. And even Gordon could redeem himself, Burke added, if he came to "meditate on his Talmud, until he learns a conduct more becoming to his birth and parts, and not so disgraceful to the ancient religion to which he has become a proselyte."[27]

Unlike Burke, who was respectful of Judaism as a religion if not of Jews, his friend David Hume was notably skeptical of religion but sympathetic to Jews, both as individuals and as representatives of the trades for which they were vilified. In his *History of England*, he condemned the treatment meted out to Jews in the early history of the country as a reflection of "the low state of commerce" at the time. Subjected to "barefaced acts of tyranny and oppression," they were deprived of the protection of law, abandoned to the "immeasurable rapacity" of the king, and finally plundered and banished from the kingdom.[28] Adam Smith, a friend of both Hume and Burke, also related the prejudice against Jews to the "mean and despicable idea" the English had of merchants and commerce. Confined to trade because they were not permitted to own land, the Jews were "grievously oppressed and consequently the progress of opulence [was] greatly retarded."[29]

Not all Englishmen, then or later, agreed with Hume and Smith (and Burke as well) that commerce was a civilizing, humanizing, and socially desirable activity, and thus that Jews engaged in that activity were worthy of respect and citizenship. William Cobbett, the populist journalist in the early nineteenth-century, notoriously did not. The "Poor Man's Friend," as he liked to think of himself (and as he entitled his journal), praised the Czar for banishing the Jews and suggested, only semi-facetiously, that the same should be done in England. More often he simply used "Jew" as an invective. Jews were oppressors of the poor—money-lenders, jobbers (middle-men), usurers—and foreigners and blasphemers to boot. When he wanted to castigate Quakers, he derided them as "broad-brimmed Jews" or "buttonless Jews."[30]

Thomas Carlyle had much the same view of Jews—and of the political economy with which he identified them. On one occasion, standing on Hyde Park corner before the grand house of Rothschild, he was reminded of the story told about King John, who, in 1210, arrested all wealthy Jews and demanded a ransom for their release. When one Jew refused to pay his ransom, the king ordered that one of his teeth be pulled out every day until he paid it. (The Jew succumbed after seven of his teeth had been pulled.) Carlyle imagined a latter-day King John demanding of Rothschild that he repay to the state some of the millions he had nefariously acquired, and inflicting upon him some more benign torture than the pulling of teeth—a twist of the wrist, perhaps, until those millions were yielded. James Froude, Carlyle's friend (and future biographer), who was with him during this episode, commented upon Carlyle's "true Teutonic aversion for that unfortunate race."[31]*

When the question of citizenship arose in 1830, it was against a different social background. Carlyle, Cobbett, and others of like mind knew that they were resisting the "spirit of the age." Trade and commerce were no longer invidious occupations, and Jews were not necessarily villains or pariahs. The Jewish question had a different quality in part because the Jewish population was different. Immigration had petered out, and the Jewish community was small and stable; in 1815, it numbered 20,000-30,000, two-thirds in London; in mid-century 35,000, again mainly in London. There were fewer conspicuously poor and foreign Jews, and more conspicuously respectable and affluent ones—not only such notables as the Rothschilds, Goldsmids, and Montefiores, but also businessmen, writers, scientists, and professionals of all kinds. Even some of the more celebrated converts from Judaism, like the economist David Ricardo and, of course, Benjamin Disraeli, made no secret of their Jewish origins and suffered no ill-effects as a result.

---

* Eliot was an admirer of Carlyle, of the early Carlyle (*Sartor Resartus*), however, rather than the later (the *Latter-Day Pamphlets*)—of his spirit, she said, although not necessarily his politics. "When he is saying the very opposite of what we think, he says it so finely, . . . he appeals so constantly to our sense of the manly and the truthful, that we are obliged to say 'Hear! hear!' to the writer before we can give the decorous 'Oh! oh!' to his opinions."[32] This review appeared in 1855, about the same time as Lewes's biography of Goethe, which was proofread by Carlyle and dedicated to him.

As Jews became more respectable and acceptable, so they also became more likely candidates for citizenship. In fact, they were already citizens, to a degree. Jews born in Britain were entitled to vote in local and parliamentary elections, provided only that they met the property qualifications required of all citizens. The restrictions on foreign-born Jews were eased with the passage of a naturalization bill in 1826 (another Jew Bill) abolishing the religious oath; that bill went through both houses without serious controversy in or outside of Parliament. What native-born Jews (together with Dissenters and Catholics) still lacked was admission to public offices, universities, and Parliament, all of which required the taking of the religious oath. The original version of the bill repealing the Test and Corporation Acts in 1828 would have eliminated these restrictions on Jews as well as Dissenters and Catholics. A bishop in the House of Lords inserted the words "on the true faith of a Christian" in the required declaration, thus allowing for the emancipation of Dissenters and, the following year, Catholics, but not Jews.

In 1830 Thomas Babington Macaulay entered the fray with his maiden speech in Parliament supporting a bill for the elimination of the "civil disabilities of Jews"—in effect, their emancipation on a par with Dissenters and Catholics. That bill failed, but an expanded version of his speech, in the *Edinburgh Review* the following year brought his message to a large and receptive audience. Appealing, he said, not to sentiment or philosophy but only to common sense, he sought to expose the "absurdity and injustice" of the reasons commonly invoked to disqualify Jews. To the argument that the constitution was and should remain Christian, he replied that the proposal was "not that the Jews should legislate for a Christian community, but that a legislature composed of

Christians and Jews should legislate for a community composed of Christians and Jews."[33] And to the assertion that the right to property carried with it no right to political power, he pointed out that the security of property rested with government, and government meant political power. "Why a man should be less fit to exercise those powers because he wears a beard, because he does not eat ham, because he goes to the synagogue on Saturdays instead of going to the church on Sundays, we cannot conceive."[34]

Reintroduced in 1833, the bill passed in the reformed House of Commons but was defeated in the Lords. Renewed attempts in the following decades met with similar results. Short of full emancipation, however, Jews came to enjoy greater respect and public recognition. In 1837, Moses Montefiore, president of the Jewish communal organization and a strictly observant Orthodox Jew (he traveled with his own *shochet,* who supervised the ritual slaughter), was appointed sheriff of London and knighted by the Queen on her first visit to the City. In 1841, Isaac Goldsmid, a Reformed Jew, received a baronetcy, as did Montefiore five years later. The office of sheriff was opened to Jews in 1833 and other municipal offices in 1845. The great challenge came in 1847 when Lionel Rothschild was elected to Parliament by the City of London but could not be seated because he refused to take the oath "on the true faith of a Christian."

A Jewish Disabilities Bill introduced late that year produced speeches that were all the more memorable because they were not entirely predictable. Much of the debate centered on the question of whether the admission of Jews to Parliament was compatible with a Christian constitution and nation. Gladstone spoke in favor of the bill, in spite of his own strong theological commitments to Christianity, on the grounds that a few Jews in the House of Commons could hardly alter its essentially Christian character. Disraeli, with his customary flair for paradox, insisted that England was indeed a Christian nation, and for that very reason it should welcome Jews who were, after all, "the authors of your religion." "If religion is a security for righteous conduct, you have that security in the instance of the Jews, who profess a true religion."[35]

More paradoxical was the speech by Lord Ashley (later Lord Shaftesbury), the great Evangelical and social reformer. Opposing the bill because he believed it diminished the Christian nature of the state, he did so reluctantly and agonizingly, and only after the most laudatory tributes to Jews.

> The Jews were a people of very powerful intellect, of cultivated minds, and with habits of study that would defy the competition of the most indefatigable German . . . [They] presented . . . in our day, in proportion to their numbers, a far larger list of men of genius and learning than could be exhibited by any Gentile country. Music, poetry, medicine, astronomy, occupied their attention, and in all they were more than a match for their competitors. . . . They exhibited a greater desire and a greater fitness to re-enter the general family of mankind . . . [and] merited every concession that could contribute to their honour and comfort.[36]

The Jews "merited every concession," in short, except their admission to Parliament.

The debate was serious and respectful, with few anti-Semitic overtones. Passed by the House of Commons with a comfortable majority, the bill was rejected by the Lords, where the Bishops played a dominant role. In the following years, the City of London continued to elect Rothschild, with the same futile result. Fourteen such bills were introduced, approved by the Commons but not by the Lords. In 1858, three years after a Jew had been elected Lord Mayor of London, a compromise was reached permitting each House to determine its own form of oath. Taking the new oath "So help me Jehovah," Lionel Rothschild became the first Jewish Member of Parliament. The 1858 measure applied to him specifically. The following year his brother, Mayer Rothschild, was seated after the passage of a similar resolution regarding all Jews. In 1866 the House of Common fixed upon its required oath, "So help me God."

English Jews were thus admitted to full citizenship, not as individuals who had to prove their Englishness by denying their identity as Jews, but as Englishmen who were also Jews—many of whom, indeed, were observant Jews, practicing just that "exclusive" religion which on the continent condemned them as "a nation within a nation." Moreover, they were admitted to citizenship in a country that, so far from becoming secular and repudiating its Christian identity, retained its established church while respecting the religious diversity of its citizenry. This tolerant attitude was not significantly affected by the admission of new immigrants from Germany, Poland, and Holland in the third quarter of the century, bringing the number of English Jews to 65,000 by 1880. Largely Ashkenazi, somewhat poorer but not destitute (the Jewish Board of Guardians established in 1859 assumed responsibility for the welfare of the poorer Jews), they also included some well-educated refugees who had been implicated in the German revolution of 1848.*

The generational change in the attitude towards Jews was symbolized by the Arnolds, father and son. Thomas Arnold, the master of Rugby, vigorously opposed the Jewish emancipation bills of the 1830s. Protesting against the "low Jacobinical notion of citizenship," that a man acquires a right to it by the accident of his English birth or the payment of taxes, he declared England a Christian country where only Christians had a claim to political rights. Thus Catholics and Nonconformists, who were Christians, might be deemed citizens, but not Jews. "The Jews are strangers in England, and have no more claim to legislate for it than a lodger has to share with the landlord in the management of his house."[38] Thirty-five years later, in *Culture and Anarchy*, Matthew Arnold took a quite different view of the relative merits of Jews and Nonconformists as citizens. Taking issue with Nonconformists who had principled objections to any religious establishment, Matthew Arnold insisted that it was only within an establishment that the human spirit could be cultivated. Because Nonconformists lacked any establishment or even any respect for establishment, they could produce no "men of national mark," whereas Jews and Catholics could produce such men because both

---

* In *Daniel Deronda*, Eliot alluded to the improvement in the condition of English Jews in the course of the century. Mr. Ram, the Jewish clerk in the bookstore, was a crabbed figure, having experienced as a child "the poverty and contempt which were the common heritage of most English Jews seventy years ago"—and which were conspicuously not the condition of the Jews in the novel.[37]

rested on establishments—not national ones, to be sure, but cosmopolitan ones.[39]*

In fact, the Protestant culture itself—Nonconformist as well as Anglican—facilitated the acceptance of Jews, not as strangers in the land, as Thomas Arnold thought, but as rightful residents and citizens. The daily reading of the Bible, the Old Testament and the New, served to abate the traditional animus toward Jews who were, after all, the "people of the Bible." Similarly, the proselytizing efforts of the Evangelicals, the societies for the conversion of Jews, had the effect of reminding Christians of their origins, thus elevating Judaism as a religion and making Jews worthy of respect and even reverence. Indeed, some of the Evangelicals went so far in their tributes to Judaism as to verge on philo-Semitism.

The case of Shaftesbury is especially interesting because of his opposition to Jewish emancipation. (He approved of the bill ten years later when he was in the House of Lords, only because he felt the Lords could no longer resist the will of the Commons. "I yield to force, not to reason," he explained.) Even as he was arguing against the political rights of Jews, he was supporting humanitarian efforts on their behalf in England and abroad. He also led the movement for the "Res-

---

* Eliot read *Culture and Anarchy* as it appeared serially in 1867-1868 and defended Arnold against her friend Frederic Harrison, whom Arnold had attacked as hostile to culture. Perhaps because she had been "warped" by reading the Germans, she told Harrison, she agreed with Arnold in regarding "culture" as "the highest mental result of past and present influences."[40] She did not comment on Arnold's view of "Hebraism and Hellenism": Hebraism overly concerned with the moral life and therefore a threat to Hellenism, the life of the mind. Given her own moral disposition, she would have seen no contradiction between the two.

toration of Jews" in Palestine—not, as a cynic might think, to remove them from England, but because he believed in the Second Coming of Christ, which required the return of the Jews to the Holy Land (and their conversion). He pursued this cause his entire life, taking the occasion of one Near Eastern crisis after another to make the case for a Jewish settlement in Palestine. In 1853, on the eve of the Crimean War, he urged Lord Palmerston, the Foreign Minister, to persuade Turkey to cede some land in Palestine to the Jews, and repeated that appeal the following year to Lord Clarendon. The Turkish empire, he wrote in his diary, was in decay. The territory occupied by Syria (including Palestine) would be assigned to some one or other, and no one had better claim to it than the Jews. "There is a country *without a nation*; and God now, in His wisdom and mercy, directs us to *a nation without a country*. His own once loved, nay, still loved people, the sons of Abraham, of Isaac, and of Jacob."[41] Those phrases, "country without a nation" and "nation without a country," have been associated with the famous Zionist slogan: "A land without a people for a people without a land."*

Shaftesbury's theological motive for the Restoration of Jews was hardly shared by his Jewish contemporaries or by later Zionists. But it was based, he repeatedly affirmed, on the highest regard for Jews, not only as potential Christians

---

* This phrase, attributed by Edward Said to Israel Zangwill in 1901, was the source of Said's charge that Zionists willfully propagated the idea that Palestine was uninhabited—that there were no "people" there. In fact, the phrase was coined by an Evangelical clergyman in 1843, who was well aware that the country was populated because he had travelled in Palestine. By "people" he, like later Zionists, meant "nation."[42]

but also as Jews. In 1847, opposing the Jewish enfranchisement bill, he assured his colleagues that he held "the very poorest Israelite with feelings akin to reverence, as one of the descendants of the most remarkable nation that had ever yet appeared on the face of the earth—one of the forefathers of those who were yet to play the noblest part in the history of mankind."[43] Twenty-one years later, he recalled that event. "The Jewish question has now been settled," he reported to Gladstone, who had just assumed the prime ministership; Jews could now sit in both houses of Parliament. He himself had resisted their admission not because he was "adverse to the descendants of Abraham, of whom our Blessed Lord came according to the flesh," but because he objected to the way that admission had been effected. But all that, he said, was of the past. He now implored Gladstone to take the opportunity to show regard for "God's ancient people" by giving a peerage to "a noble member of the House of Israel," Sir Moses Montefiore. "It would be a glorious day for the House of Lords when that grand old Hebrew were enrolled on the lists of the hereditary legislators of England."[44] If it is ironic that Shaftesbury should be proposing to elevate Montefiore to the Lords, having once denied Rothschild a seat in the Commons, it is also ironic that Disraeli, whom Shaftesbury had earlier approached with the same suggestion, felt that for obvious reasons he could not act upon it, while Gladstone, who had no such excuse, failed to do so without explanation (after inquiring, however, about the size of Montefiore's fortune and whether he had children).

Although Disraeli played no part in Shaftesbury's Restoration movement, he was no less enthusiastic for the cause. A young friend of Disraeli's, Lord Stanley (the son of the leader of the Tories, later the 15th Earl of Derby), recalled a conversation in 1851 when Disraeli spoke movingly about the return of the Jews to their homeland and even suggested the means for achieving it. The country, Disraeli pointed out, had excellent natural resources; all that was wanted was labor and ownership of the soil. The former would be provided by Jews, the latter by the Rothschilds and other "Hebrew capitalists" who would purchase the land from the Turkish government, which was desperate for money. Such ideas, Disraeli assured Stanley, were widespread among the Jews, and the man who carried them out would be "the next Messiah, the true Saviour of his people." Recording this conversation in his diary four years later, Stanley observed that Disraeli was completely in earnest and that this was the only occasion when he showed signs of real emotion.[45]

Much later, in 1878 when the Congress of Berlin convened to solve the "Eastern Question" that had precipitated the Prusso-Turkish war, rumors spread that Disraeli (Lord Beaconsfield, as he then was) was proposing a protectorate over Syria, one of the provisions of which would provide for the return of Jews to Palestine. The rumors were unfounded, but they were picked up by newspapers as a solution not only to the Eastern Question but also to the Jewish Question. An English weekly, the *Spectator*, rebuked Disraeli for not supporting the plan. "If he had freed the Holy Land and restored the Jews, as he might have done

instead of pottering about Romania and Afghanistan, he
would have died Dictator."[46]

Quite apart from anything Disraeli did, or failed to do,
to "solve" the Jewish question, in his very person he drew
attention to that question. Indeed, for many Englishmen he
personified Jewishness. A philo-Semite by conviction, he was
a Semite by birth, and that birthright was not negated (in Disraeli's view or that of his countrymen) by the fact that he had
been baptized at the age of twelve, shortly before he would
have qualified for the Bar Mitzvah rite.* He deliberately exag-
gerated his Semitic appearance by having his black hair set in
elaborate ringlets (it was dyed in his later years by his wife),
and by an unconventional attire that made him seem even
more foreign. And he prided himself on being of the Jewish
"race"—his word, not his enemies'. From his earliest years,
he aspired to the highest office of state, and as he climbed that
"greasy pole" to the top, he went out of his way to remind
his colleagues and constituents of his heritage—and readers
as well, for that was the theme of some of his best and most
memorable novels.

It was also the theme of one of his least distinguished
novels. In 1828, when he was twenty-four, he conceived the
idea of *The Wondrous Tale of Alroy*. Three years later, during
his first visit to Jerusalem, he was reminded of that "gorgeous
incident in the annals of that sacred and romantic people

---

* Isaac D'Israeli, a Reformed Jew, had his children baptized only because
he did not want to serve as warden in his synagogue. But he himself was
not converted, did not change his name or conceal his Jewishness, and
enjoyed such social amenities as membership in the Athenaeum and the
friendship of Byron, Southey, Scott, and other literary eminences.

from whom I derive by blood and name."[47]* The novel, he confided to his diary, portrayed his "ideal ambition."[49] That ambition, pursued by the hero of the novel (a much idealized version of the real twelfth-century David Alroy), was a "national existence" in the "Land of Promise," the land that represented "all we have yearned after, all we have fought for, our beauteous country, our holy creed, our simple manners, and our ancient customs."[50]

In 1833, when *Alroy* appeared, Disraeli was a failed contender for a seat in Parliament. Fourteen years, six novels, and several elections later, he was on the Front Bench, delivering his speech in support of the Jewish emancipation bill. *Tancred*, the last of the trilogy of novels that included *Coningsby* and *Sybil*, was published that year. It was the most romantic, mystical, messianic, and Jewish of Disraeli's novels—and, as he said toward the end of his life, the favorite of all his novels.[51] It was in *Tancred* that Sidonia propounded the doctrine, "All is race; there is no other truth."[52] Sidonia had appeared earlier, in *Coningsby*, as the Rothschild-like banker, "lord and master of the money-market of the world, and of course virtually lord and master of everything else"—

---

* "Blood and name"—Disraeli romanticized both. In a memoir prefacing the collected works of his father, he claimed descent from a family that had been expelled from Spain in 1492 and had settled in Venice, where they deliberately, he said, assumed the name Disraeli, a name that had never been used before, "in order that their race might be for ever recognized." In fact, there is no evidence that the family had been Spanish, and the family name—"Israeli" before his father changed it to "D'Israeli"—was a common Arabic name applied to Jews in Spain and the Levant. Even "Disraeli" was not unique. There was a Protestant family of that name in London during the eighteenth century; the last member, a Benjamin Disraeli, was a rich Dublin moneylender, who had no connection with our Benjamin Disraeli.[48]

a scion of that "unmixed race" that was the "aristocracy of Nature."[53] Tancred, the hero of the novel, was not Jewish. He was of an entirely different aristocracy: the only son of the Duke of Bellamont, who was the virtual "head of the English nobility."[54]* Repelled by the materialistic, soulless culture in England, Tancred defied his father by making a pilgrimage to Jerusalem to "penetrate the great Asian mystery."[56] In Jerusalem, he discovered that it was not enough to be in the land of the Saviour to know His will, that there was "a qualification of blood as well as of locality necessary for this communion, and that the favoured votary must not only kneel in the Holy Land but be of the holy race."[57] Eva (the Jewess), put it more sharply. "We agree that half Christendom worships a Jewess, and the other half a Jew. . . . Which do you think should be the superior race, the worshipped or the worshipper?"[58]

Willfully provocative in his person as in his novels, Disraeli was sometimes greeted on the hustings with the familiar gibes: "Shylock," "Old Clothes," "Judas," "Bring a bit of pork for the Jew."[59] Daniel O'Connell, the Irish Radical leader, said that there were "respectable Jews," but Disraeli was not one of them: "He has just the qualities of the impenitent thief on the Cross"; this was his genealogy and his "infa-

---

* The origin of the name Tancred was not explained in the novel. It was implied, however, in the description of an ancestor of the family as "one of the most distinguished knights in the third crusade, having saved the life of Coeur de Lion at the siege of Ascalon."[55] But the historic Tancred was a knight not in the third crusade but in the first, a leader in the conquest of Jerusalem in 1099. Theodor Herzl, as a student in Vienna, had been inducted into a German nationalist fraternity under the name Tancred—this after the ritual of a saber duel. He later suggested that duelling be officially accredited in the state of Israel, as a token of the aristocratic and nationalist spirit of the new country.

mous distinction."[60] And Carlyle, with his "true Teutonic aversion" to Jews, despised this "Pinchbeck-Hebrew, almost professedly a Son of Belial," a "cursed old Jew, not worth his weight in cold bacon."[61] What was remarkable was that in spite of these old prejudices (and in spite of Disraeli himself, some of his admirers thought), Disraeli did achieve the ultimate goal of political power. After the conclusion of the Congress of Berlin, Bismarck paid tribute to *der alte Jude, das ist der Mann.*" Historians and biographers continue to be intrigued by *der alte Jude,* and still more intrigued by the country and the party (the Conservative Party) that gave him that eminence.[62]

The more familiar literary figure of the Jew was not an Alroy or Sidonia who wanted to restore his "race" to its proper historic role, but a Fagin who represented that race at its worse. Dickens, it was said at the time, was a "low writer"; he wrote about low subjects for a low audience.[63]* Fagin was a low character indeed, a criminal and corrupter of children as well as an exploiter of the poor. A quarter of a century later, in a revised edition of *Oliver Twist,* Dickens tried to soften, ever so slightly, this image. Responding to the appeal by a Jewish woman (the wife of his banker with whom he had

---

* Queen Victoria, reading the book over the objections of her mother (who disapproved not only of "low" books but of all "light" books), found *Oliver Twist* "excessively interesting" and recommended it to her Prime Minister, Lord Melbourne. Melbourne confessed he could not get beyond the first chapters. "It's all among Workhouses, and Coffin Makers, and Pickpockets," he protested. "I shouldn't think it would tend to raise morals; I don't like that low debasing view of mankind. . . . I don't like them in reality, and therefore I don't wish them represented."[64]

good relations) to "atone for a great wrong on a whole but scattered nation," he substituted the name "Fagin" for the invidious words "the Jew." Two years later, he performed a more serious act of atonement in *Our Mutual Friend*. His last completed novel, published in 1865, it featured Riah, an old "gentle" Jew, an altogether admirable character, in contrast to his "Christian master," Fledgeby, "the meanest cur existing," who compounded his villainy by concealing his ownership of the money-lending firm, thus obliging his assistant Riah to take responsibility for his evil deeds.[65]

Dickens's Jews, for good or bad, were of the lower classes. Anthony Trollope's were unmistakably upper-class. A staunch Liberal, Trollope was said to have developed a special animus against Jews because of his intense dislike for Disraeli, who was not only a Jew but a Tory, and, to make matters worse, a novelist who received larger advances for his novels than Trollope did for his. A money-lender in *Barchester Towers* was called Sidonia, and an especially unprincipled Tory politician in *The Prime Minister* and *Phineas Finn* was clearly patterned on Disraeli himself. His political novels especially, the Palliser novels, had a fair number of disagreeable Jews—not lowly pawn-brokers and money-lenders, but wealthy financiers and speculators.[*]

Like Dickens, Trollope was somewhat repentant in his later years. *The Way We Live Now*, published in 1875, was the most bitter and deeply pessimistic of his novels, an expo-

---

[*] A conspicuous exception was Madame Goesler in *Phineas Finn*. The daughter of a German Jewish attorney and the widow of a Jewish banker, she was one of the most intelligent and high-minded of Trollope's characters. One critic has described her as "the most perfect gentleman" in his novels—than which, for Trollope, there could be no higher praise (although he would surely not have applied the word "gentleman" to a lady).[66]

sure of the mercenary values of the new commercial society, afflicting almost all the characters and all aspects of life, including love and marriage. Among its many villains, the worst was the dishonest speculator Augustus Melmotte, who was only ambiguously Jewish; he was assumed to be Jewish because his wife, who was vaguely East European, was thought to be so. Melmotte's disagreeable associate, Cohenlupe, was unmistakeably Jewish. On the other hand, Ezekiel Brehgert, who "went to a synagogue on a Saturday" and was "absolutely a Jew," was an honest banker and a thoroughly honorable man. This "old fat Jew" proposed marriage to a "Christian lady," who accepted him, over the objections of her parents, for the most materialistic reasons. Her father, the squire, was a disagreeable bully and her mother was vapid and fatuous. "It's unnatural," her mother said of the marriage. "I'm sure there's something in the Bible against it. You never would read your Bible, or you wouldn't be going to do this." Brehgert, on the other hand, was decent and intelligent. "I behaved like a gentleman," he said, explaining that he had to withdraw his proposal of marriage because he could not provide the magnificent house she had made a condition of marriage.[67] He was, indeed, the only gentleman in the novel.

By the third quarter of the century, the kind of anti-Semitism familiar in Victorian literature, represented by usurious pawnbrokers and unscrupulous financiers, was much abated. The stereotypes and prejudices remained, in society and in the culture. But they were less vehement, less taken for granted. As the political aspect of the Jewish question had been amicably resolved, so, too, the cultural and social aspects had been not resolved, to be sure, but much alleviated. When *Daniel Deronda* was published, the year after *The Way We Live Now*, the reader would not have been surprised to encounter a Jewish hero who was also a gentleman. What did surprise the public, and what made the book so controversial, was the fact that an "English gentleman," as Deronda's mother described him, was pleased to discover that he was Jewish and proud of his "race," and that he chose to leave England and join his people in Palestine.

Even more surprising was the fact that the novel was written not by a Jew or even a converted Jew (converted from or to Judaism), but by a proper English Christian lady. As the English had confronted the challenge of the Jewish question, so George Eliot had as well. In a sense, *Daniel Deronda* was her "solution" to that historic question.

II.

GEORGE ELIOT'S INITIATION *into* "THE JEWISH QUESTION"

Before encountering "the Jewish question," George Eliot had to work her way through "the Christian question," and then, more boldly, through "the religious question."

There was no "question," of course, for the child Mary Anne, born on November 22, 1819, the youngest of five children (two half-siblings and three siblings) of a respectable estate-manager in Warwickshire. Her father, Robert Evans, a low-church Anglican, observed the religious conventions of his church and community. If he thought about them at all, it was to be wary of anything smacking of "enthusiasm," such as the Methodism to which his brother had been converted. He could not have known that that it was a different variety of enthusiasm he was exposing his daughter to when he sent her, at the age of eight, to a boarding school, where an Evangelical teacher instilled in her the habit of the daily reading of the Bible and study of the Scriptures. Transferred to another school four years later, she encountered a more rigorous Calvinistic form of Evangelicalism, which, as she later explained, sought to "shape this anomalous English-Christian life of ours into some consistency with the spirit and simple verbal tenor of the New Testament." She was distressed to recall the "stern, ascetic hard views" that had made her censorious, on one occasion, of a deceased minister who was known to be something of a tippler.[1] Returning home at the age of sixteen to tend to her father after her mother died (this was the end of her formal schooling), she brought with her that religious and moral earnestness. Three years later, on her first visit to London with her brother (the only member of the family with whom she was close), she refused to accompany him to the theater, spending the evening instead reading Josephus's *History of the Jews*.

Mary Ann (as she then signed her name) was about twenty when her intellectual curiosity and omniverous reading began to wean her from this mode of Evangelicalism.[*] She became enamored of the romantic poets, who were hardly conducive to a stern asceticism, read Newman's *Lyra Apostolica* and *Tracts for the Times*, which were heretical for an Evangelical and unsettling for any Anglican, and developed an interest in the sciences, some of which (geology, most notably) cast doubt on the literal truth of the Scriptures, while others (mathematics, astronomy, chemistry) enlarged her universe well beyond the range of religion. She also started to take lessons in Italian and German, which opened up still newer vistas of mind and spirit. (Latin, Greek, and French she had studied in school; Hebrew came later.)

A more decisive rupture came late in 1841, when she and her father moved to the neighboring town of Coventry. She

---

[*] It is awkward to first-name Eliot, in this period of her life, while surnaming the men. But this is the convention, and anything else (Evans or Mary Ann Evans) seems pompous and contrived. I lapse into Eliot, even in this early period, when the context calls for it.

then met the Brays and was introduced to their circle of intellectuals and free-thinkers. Caroline Bray's brother, Charles Hennell, was the author of *An Inquiry into the Origins of Christianity,* which was meant to provide a theological rationale for Unitarianism. Charles Bray went further, his recently published *Philosophy of Necessity* making the positivist case for agnosticism. The Brays and their acquaintances did not so much indoctrinate their young friend as expose her to modes of belief—and unbelief—that helped subvert not only Evangelicalism but Christianity as well. In the process, they also introduced her to some of the sources of Jewish law and learning: the Talmud, medieval Jewish sages and commentators like Maimonides, and, not least, the Higher Biblical criticism that was flourishing in Germany and was radically reinterpreting both the Old and the New Testaments.

On January 2, 1842, as if fulfilling a new year's resolution, Mary Ann refused for the first time to accompany her father to church. Persisting in this act of rebellion, much to the distress of her father, she wrote him a letter assuring him that she had no intention of joining the Unitarians or any other Dissenting sect (which apparently was the worst of his fears). She then went on to describe her own religious views, which were even more troubling:

> I regard these writings [the Jewish and Christian scriptures] as histories consisting of mingled truth and fiction, and while I admire and cherish much of what I believe to have been the moral teaching of Jesus himself, I consider the system of doctrines built upon the facts of his life and drawn as to its materials from Jewish notions to be most dishonourable to God and most pernicious in its influence on individual and social happiness. . . . Such being

my very strong convictions . . . I could not without vile
hypocrisy and a miserable truckling to the smile of the
world for the sake of my supposed interests, profess to
join in worship which I wholly disapprove.[2]

After other futile exchanges between father and daughter, and
threats on his part to leave Coventry and remove her from his
household, a compromise was arranged: she would accompany him to church, but could think whatever she liked during the service.

Mary Ann thought and did as she liked to such good effect
that, at the age of twenty-three, she undertook the ambitious
project (initially meant for Hennell's wife) of translating
David Strauss's *Das Leben Jesu*, which had been published
in Germany half-a-dozen years earlier. It was a considerable
job of translation—a two-volume work of 1500 pages, with
abundant quotations in Latin, Greek, and Hebrew.* *The Life
of Jesus* appeared in 1846, and although Mary Ann Evans's
name was not on the title page, it was well known in her
circle, establishing her credentials not only as translator, but
also as an intellectual and a freethinker.

With the Strauss translation out of the way, Mary Ann had
more time for reading. A list of the authors of books men-

---

* Eliot's translation was of the fourth edition of Strauss's book. The second
and third editions, in 1837 and 1838, were more conciliatory. The fourth,
in 1839, returned to the more radical tone of the first edition. Eliot must
have had assistance in translating the Hebrew passages, because it was only
later that she started to study Hebrew seriously.

tioned in her letters in the course of only a few years is awe-
some: Shakespeare, Milton, Rousseau, Wordsworth, Carlyle,
Goethe, Saint-Simon, Lamartine, George Sand, Dickens,
Thackeray, and Disraeli, among others. In the light of *Daniel
Deronda* published almost thirty years later, her comments on
Disraeli's *Tancred* are most intriguing.[3] That novel, exploring
"the great Asian mystery" of the Jewish "race," provoked
Eliot to some sharp reflections on Judaism, a subject she had
obviously encountered in her translation of Strauss but that
she had not commented on in her own voice.

Tancred, she complained to a friend early in 1848, was
very thin, inferior to both *Coningsby* and *Sybil*. Disraeli was
"unquestionably an able man" and she respected some of his
principles, but not his "Young Englandism" and still less his
theory about race, which had "not a leg to stand on." Disraeli attributed the superiority of the Jews to the fact that
they were so pure a race, but it was just this purity that led
to the deterioration of races. "Extermination up to a certain
point seems to be the law for the inferior races—for the rest,
fusion both for physical and moral ends." Just as privileged
classes tended to degenerate from continual intermarriage, so
did races. The case of the Negroes, she confessed, puzzled her:
"All the other races seem plainly destined to extermination or
fusion not excepting even the 'Hebrew Caucasion.' But the
Negroes are too important, physiologically and geographi-
cally, for one to think of their extermination, while the repulsion between them and the other races seems too strong for
fusion to take place to any great extent." On one small point,
she agreed with Disraeli: the oriental races were superior in
respect to their beautiful clothes and agreeable manners. But
she saw no reason to ascribe any superiority to the Jews.

The fellowship of race, to which D'Israeli [*sic*] so exult-
ingly refers the munificence of Sidonia, is so evidently an
inferior impulse which must ultimately be superseded that
I wonder even he, Jew as he is, dares to boast of it. My
Gentile nature kicks most resolutely against any assumption of superiority in the Jews, and is almost ready to echo
Voltaire's vituperation. I bow to the supremacy of Hebrew
poetry, but much of their early mythology and almost all
their history is utterly revolting. Their stock has produced
a Moses and a Jesus, but Moses was impregnated with
Egyptian philosophy and Jesus is venerated and adored by
us only for that wherein He transcended or resisted Judaism. The very exaltation of their idea of a national deity
into a spiritual monotheism seems to have been borrowed
from the other oriental tribes. Everything *specifically* Jewish is of a low grade.[4]

One biographer of Eliot, confessing that he winced at the
racial theories and intimations of anti-Semitism in this letter,
explained that she was using "race" in the familiar sense of
the time, and that the word "extermination" did not have the
meaning it has since acquired, implying only intermarriage
(the "fusion" of races) or the natural dying out of races.[5] In
fact, she was only following Disraeli (and the Victorians generally) in equating race with what we would now call ethnic-
ity. Disraeli himself always insisted that Jews were a race over
and above the Jewish religion that also defined them. Lady
Rothschild recalled Disraeli saying to her, "All is race, not
religion—remember that."[6]

Mary Ann's criticisms of Disraeli recall not the "vituperation" of Voltaire, but the theories of Strauss, whose *Life of
Jesus* she had finished translating two years earlier. She had

come a long way since she had started that translation. "But surely," she had written, midway in her work, "Christianity with its Hebrew retrospect and millennial hopes, the heroism and Divine sorrow of its founder and all its glorious army of martyrs might supply and has supplied a strong impulse not only to poetry but to all the fine arts."[7] By the time she concluded that work, her immersion in Strauss had given her a more acerbic view of both Christianity and Judaism—and of religion in general.

Strauss's influence may also be seen in the reviews she contributed to a local radical paper owned by Bray. She wrote approvingly of two books on Christianity by the French anti-clerical historian Jules Michelet, as well as the semi-autobiographical novel *Nemesis of Faith* by James Anthony Froude, which was regarded as sufficiently heretical to be publicly burned at the Oxford college where Froude was a fellow. Almost the last task she started, while still living with her father, was a translation of Spinoza's *Tractatus Theologico-Politicus,* a project she abandoned after a few months explaining that a translation alone was insufficient to convey the essence of this man who "says from his own soul what all the world is saying by rote."[8*]

After her father's death in May 1849, Mary Ann's first act of liberation was to accompany the Brays on a tour abroad, remaining in Geneva, on her own, for about eight months. Upon her return the publisher John Chapman, contemplating the purchase of the *Westminster Review*, asked her to review

---

* Although she did not personally meet Lewes until later, she would have known of him (he was acquainted with others in the Bray circle), and she may well have read his article on Spinoza, which originally appeared in the *Westminster Review* in 1843 and was reissued as a pamphlet in 1849, about the time she abandoned her own project of translation.

a book by his friend William Mackay, a disciple of Strauss, with the formidable title, *The Progress of the Intellect, as Exemplified in the Religious Development of the Greeks and Hebrews*. Her fifteen-page review so impressed him that he offered her the assistant-editorship of the *Review*, with primary responsibility for the section on French and German literature. She ended up virtually editing the magazine as well as writing a dozen or so reviews, some of essay-length.

As she had earlier found a spiritual home in Coventry among the Brays and their circle, so now, in the early 1850s, she became part of a larger and livelier circle in London centered upon Chapman and the *Westminster Review*. The Chapman house, where the *Review* had its offices and where Mary Ann lived as a boarder, became a meeting place for radicals and intellectuals of every variety—utilitarians, positivists, evolutionists, feminists, agnostics. In this congenial atmosphere, Mary Ann lived, worked, and wrote for four years. In October 1851 she met George Lewes (they were introduced by Chapman, in a bookstore, appropriately), with whom she soon formed a special friendship. Encouraged by him, she undertook another ambitious project, the translation of Ludwig Feuerbach's *Das Wesen des Christenthums*, which had appeared in Germany in 1841.

To a friend Eliot wrote, after she finished the translation: "With the ideas of Feuerbach I everywhere agree, but of course I should, of myself, alter the phraseology considerably."[9] One wonders whether she would have altered the phraseology of the passages toward the end of that book, in which Feuerbach, affirming the idea of love as the essence of humanity, explained that marriage, the love of man and woman, needed no sanctification by any external authority, religious or secular. "Marriage—we mean, of course, marriage as the free bond of love—is sacred in itself, by the very nature of the union which is therein effected." A footnote elaborated upon this: "Yes, only as the free bond of love; for a marriage the bond of which is merely an external restriction, not the voluntary, contented self-restriction of love, in short, a marriage which is not spontaneously concluded, spontaneously willed, self-sufficing, is not a true marriage, and therefore not a truly moral marriage."[10]

The Essence of Christianity, translated by Marian Evans (as her name appeared on the title page), was published in July 1854.* A few days later she and Lewes embarked together, in the "free bond of love," on a trip to Germany—their honeymoon, in effect. The six-month trip was an immersion in German culture. In Cologne, they had breakfast with Strauss, a not altogether satisfactory meeting because of a language difficulty; in Frankfurt they visited the house where Goethe was born (Lewes was writing a biography of him), as well as the Jewish quarter (which Eliot was to revisit later and which was to appear in a scene in *Daniel Deronda*); in Weimar

---

* Eliot's translations of both Strauss and Feuerbach survive in the most recent editions of both works. *The Essence of Christianity* includes a foreword and an introduction by two distinguished modern theologians, Reinhold Niebuhr and Karl Barth. The last paragraph of Niebuhr's foreword pays tribute to Eliot:

> "The present translation of *The Essence of Christianity* was made by George Eliot (Marian Evans) and published first in 1854. Like Feuerbach and many other contemporaries, in revolt against what seemed a repressive orthodoxy and against the equation of the church with established social order, she sought to retain the ethos of Christianity without its faith, its humanism without its theism, its hope for man without its hope for the sovereignty of God."[11]

they became friendly with Liszt (also mentioned in *Daniel Deronda*) and attended several private piano performances by him; in Berlin they found themselves in a lively community of writers and artists and were much moved by a performance of Lessing's *Nathan the Wise*, an ardent plea for religious toleration whose hero was modeled on Moses Mendelssohn. But above all they read and wrote. While Lewes worked on his biography of Goethe, Eliot translated Spinoza's *Ethics*, wrote several pieces for the *Westminster Review*, and read voraciously—Goethe, Schiller, Lessing, Heine, Schlegel, and German translations and commentaries on Shakespeare. This was the first of several such trips, working holidays in Germany mainly but also in France, Italy, and Switzerland. (Another meeting with Strauss in Munich in 1858 was more agreeable because Eliot's conversational German had improved.)

Thomas Carlyle and Matthew Arnold are often credited with bringing German culture to England, but a good case can be made for Eliot and Lewes—and for Eliot more than Lewes. Lewes's biography of Goethe, published in 1855, stimulated interest in a poet who was already well known, largely as a result of Carlyle's translations. But Eliot's long essay on Heine the following year in the *Westminister Review* (as well as three short articles on him in other journals) was his first introduction to the English-speaking world. And it was Eliot alone whose translations of Strauss and Feuerbach brought the Young Hegelians to England, introducing an iconoclastic mode of thought more philosophical and radical than the familiar varieties of English agnosticism and atheism.

What Eliot did not bring to England from Germany was the Young Hegelian view of the Jewish question. She probably did not read the essays of that title by Bauer and Marx (their names do not appear in her writings or letters). But she could hardly have ignored the discussions of Judaism in the works of Strauss and Feuerbach which she had translated. Yet she made no mention of them. Nor were there more than a few passing references to Jews or Judaism in the scores of articles she wrote in the 1850s. Nor did Spinoza intrude into those articles, although she was then working on her translation of the *Ethics*. (The translation was completed in 1856 but was not published because of a disagreement with the publisher.)

It is also surprising that Eliot's long adulatory essay on Heine in the *Westminster Review* in January 1856 (a month before his death) should have made so little of his Jewishness. "German Wit: Heinrich Heine" went well beyond the "wit" of the title to include an account of his life and work. Yet it was neglectful of the Jewish aspect of both. Eliot identified Heine as "half a Hebrew" and his mother as "not of Hebrew but of Teutonic blood." In fact, Heine was entirely Hebrew, as was his mother. Eliot referred not to his conversion from Judaism, but to his being "united with the Lutheran Church" in order to remain resident in Berlin. "I could afterwards, as before," she quoted him, "accommodate myself, to the very enlightened Christianity, filtrated from all superstition, which could then be had in the churches of Berlin, and which was even free from the divinity of Christ, like turtle-soup without turtle." That quotation was the only indirect allusion to his conversion, leaving the impression that he had put the "half a Hebrew" part of his life well behind him.[12] Yet Jewish themes played an important part in Heine's work, and he never forgot, nor did he permit his contemporaries to forget, that he was, certainly by birth but also by spirit, more Jewish than Christian.

Seven years after Eliot's essay, another on Heine by Matthew Arnold appeared in the *Cornhill Review*. Arnold may have had Eliot in mind when he wrote, "No account of Heine is complete which does not notice the Jewish element in him." Arnold's essay was an eloquent and entirely sympathetic account of that Jewish element:

> His race he treated with the same freedom with which
> he treated everything else, but he derived a great force
> from it, and no one knew this better than he himself. He
> has excellently pointed out how in the sixteenth century
> there was a double renaissance—a Hellenic renaissance
> and a Hebrew renaissance—and how both have been
> great powers ever since. He himself had in him both the
> spirit of Greece and the spirit of Judaea; both these spirits
> reach the infinite, which is the true goal of all poetry and
> all art—the Greek spirit by beauty, the Hebrew spirit by
> sublimity. By his perfection of literary form, by his love
> of clearness, by his love of beauty, Heine is Greek; by his
> intensity, by his untamableness, by his 'longing which can-
> not be uttered,' he is Hebrew.[13]

Arnold went on to quote Heine extensively on Jews and Judaism: first, a moving story of a simple man, a Moses Lump, who had all the dignity and self-esteem of a Rothschild; and then long passages from Heine's poem on Jehuda Ben Halevy, a poet Heine identified with "the great golden age of the Arabian, Old-Spanish, Jewish school of poets."[14] Today that poem, in Heine's series called *Hebrew Melodies,* is one of the classic texts in the literature of Zionism.* It concludes with Halevy singing, "with his dying breath amid the holy ruins of Jerusalem" (dying because he has been stabbed through the heart by a passing Arab horseman), the "song of Sion." It is odd to find that poem quoted so reverently by Arnold rather than by Eliot. Twenty years later, a verse from another poem in this series, "Princess Sabbath," which Arnold had quoted in English, appeared in German as an epigraph to one of the chapters in *Daniel Deronda.*[16]

When Eliot announced that September 1856 opened a "new era" in her life, it was because it was then that she wrote her first work of fiction.[17] It was also then that she assumed a new persona, that of George Eliot. That name did not appear on the cover of *Scenes of Clerical Life* (like many novels, it was published anonymously), but it was the name she then adopted for professional and public purposes and which became the name under which she became famous.† Yet the dichotomy in her life was not nearly as sharp as she (and some biographers)

---

* Ruth Wisse, the distinguished translator and commentator on Jewish literature, recalls singing the Yiddish version of that poem, translated by the great Hebrew poet Chaim Nahman Bialik, in the Jewish school she attended in the 1940s.[15]

† Dickens prided himself on having recognized that this book, generally assumed to have been the work of a country parson, was written by a woman. His letter thanking her for the copy she had sent him was addressed to "Dear Sir." "Left to his own devices," he wrote, he would have addressed the author as a woman. "No man ever before had the art of making himself, mentally, so like a woman, since the world began."[18]

have made it appear. It was the shade of Mary Anne Evans, the enthusiastic young Evangelical, that hovered over the figure of Amos Barton and the other characters in that first novel, as in many later ones. The previous year, she had written, in the *Westminster Review*, a long critique of an eminent and, for her, an eminently disagreeable Evangelical minister, Dr. Cumming, a literal-minded interpreter of Scripture and a narrow-minded practitioner of his faith. Her fictional Evangelicals were of a different breed, practicing a high-minded and ethical religion, which, as she wrote in another of the stories in *Scenes of Clerical Life*, "brought into palpable existence and operation . . . that idea of duty, that recognition of something to be lived for beyond the mere satisfaction of self, which is to the moral life what the addition of a great central ganglion is to animal life."[19]

This insistent moral theme, "that idea of duty," pervaded all of Eliot's novels. Indeed, it became her trademark. If it sometimes seemed to displace religion or serve as a surrogate for religion, at other times it coexisted with religion or was intimately related to it. By the early 1860s, Eliot had abandoned the intransigently anti-religious views of the Young Hegelians as well as the blander humanism and agnosticism of the English Positivists. When her friend, Mme. Bodichon, once suggested that she was insufficiently respectful of religion, she hotly retorted:

> Pray don't ever ask me again not to rob a man of his religious belief, as if you thought my mind tended towards such robbery. I have too profound a conviction of the efficacy that lies in all sincere faith, and the spiritual blight that comes with No-faith, to have any negative pro-

pagandism in me. In fact, I have very little sympathy with Free-thinkers as a class, and have lost all interest in mere antagonism to religious doctrines. I care only to know, if possible, the lasting meaning that lies in all religious doctrine from the beginning till now.[20]

In 1868, writing to a positivist acquaintance to correct a mistaken impression that might have been left from their conversation, she explained that it was in her novels that her dearest beliefs were deliberately and carefully set down, so that her readers might understand and share with her "those vital elements which bind men together and give a higher worthiness to their existence." Those vital elements included religion, for, as she went on to say, she would have liked to express better what had not clearly emerged in their conversation: "my yearning affection towards the great religions of the world which have reflected the struggles and needs of mankind, with a very different degree of completeness from the shifting compromise called 'philosophical theism.'"[21]

Among those "great religions of the world" for which she was beginning to feel a special affection was Judaism. In Prague in 1858, she and Lewes had visited the Jewish burial ground and the old Synagogue. "We saw a lovely dark-eyed Jewish child here, which we were glad to kiss in all its dirt. Then came the sombre old synagugue with its smoky groins, and lamp forever burning. An intelligent Jew was our cicerone and read us some Hebrew out of the precious old book of the Law."[22] Described in exactly these words, the synagogue appeared the following year in her story, "The Lifted Veil." On later trips abroad, they sought out other synagogues; one in Leghorn reminded Eliot of a Dissenting chapel at home.[23] In Amsterdam, they looked for the Portuguese synagogue where Spinoza was nearly assassinated, but it no long existed. What they did find were three large and handsome Portuguese synagogues. Attending the evening service in one of them, Eliot observed that there were no women present but many devout men, a curious reversal, she noted, of the situation in other churches. What impressed her was the chanting and swaying of bodies, which was not beautiful but which moved her to tears as a "faint symbolism of a religion of sublime far-off memories."[24]

Portuguese Jews (or perhaps Spanish Jews, who shared the same "strongly marked type of race in their features and their peculiar garb") played a cameo part, but a vivid one, in *Romola*, published in 1863. Set in Florence in the 1490s and featuring Savonarola as one of its main characters, the novel depicted the heroine against the background of religion and politics, which was as much the drama of the story as the plight of Romola herself. Drawn at first to the charismatic figure of Savonarola and then repelled by his lack of mercy, betrayed by her husband and in despair, Romola left Florence and set out in a boat prepared to die at sea. Instead she came ashore in a small village in which a score of Jews, destitute and dying of the plague, had sought refuge after being expelled from their homeland by the Inquisition. Romola— the "Blessed Lady" or "Holy Mother," as she became known—took it upon herself to rescue what she could of the community and had the satisfaction of seeing the "Hebrew baby" she had nurtured become a "tottering tumbling Christian," baptized Benedetto.[25] (There was no mention of how the Jews felt about this baptism.) After falling sick herself, she recovered, rejuvenated in body and spirit, and returned to Florence in time to witness the death of Savonarola. An epilogue had her living with and tending to her husband's mistress and his illegitimate children, a classic end to a tale of Christian redemption.*

The decisive event in Eliot's initiation into the Jewish question was her meeting, in 1866, with Emanuel Deutsch, an assistant in the library of the British Museum. Born in Silesia, educated by his uncle, a rabbi and Talmudic scholar, before going on to the University of Berlin, Deutsch came to England in 1855 at the age of twenty-six—"a living embodiment," one commentator has it, "of Matthew Arnold's ideal union of Hebraism and Hellenism." Deutsch himself recalled his youth when "Homer and Virgil stood side by side on my boyish bookshelf with the Mishnah and the Midrash."[26] After their meeting at a friend's house, he sent Eliot the proofs of an article he had just written on the Talmud for the *Quarterly Review* and asked for her criticisms. In introducing the Talmud to an English audience, he told her, he wanted to explain "the historical 'possibility' of so much that is really fine in Christianity, to restore to Humanity one of its finest and oldest vantage grounds, and to shame shrieking fanaticism and ignorance out of its existence by a few simple facts and adages."[27] In a letter to a friend, Eliot said that she was delighted with that "glorious article on the Talmud," and with its author, "a very dear, delightful creature."[28]

---

* The Inquisition was also the background of her narrative poem *The Spanish Gypsy*, begun about the same time as *Romola* but not published until 1868. One of its curiosities was a quotation from a medieval rabbi questioning the literal truth of some biblical revelations.

This episode now seems remarkable, not only because Eliot was so taken with the article and its author, but also because the *Quarterly Review* should have chosen to publish a long essay on the Talmud and that it should have attracted so much attention, some of it favorable because it made so much of the brotherhood of Judaism and Christianity, and some critical because it recalled the persecution the Jews had endured under Christianity. That issue of the *Review* went through six editions, and Deutsch's article was translated into German, French, Swedish, Russian, Danish, and Dutch. He himself became something of a celebrity. He was invited by the Viceroy of Egypt to the ceremony at the opening of the Suez Canal, received invitations to lecture in England and America, met with Matthew Arnold to talk about Arnold's favorite subject, Hebraism and Hellenism, and was asked to dine with Disraeli, then Prime Minister.

In 1869 Deutsch visited Palestine for the first time and experienced something of an epiphany. His first letter was dated, "The East: all my wild yearnings fulfilled at last!"[29] At a lecture at the Royal Institution in London upon his return, he spoke eloquently of the Jewish faces, with "their thousand years of woe written in them," leaning against the Wailing Wall in Jerusalem. The destiny of "the once proscribed and detested Jews," he concluded, was "not yet fulfilled."[30] In his weekly visits with Eliot and Lewes, he conveyed his passion and some of his learning as well. He tutored Eliot in Hebrew, introduced her to ancient Jewish sages and modern Jewish scholarship, and spoke eloquently of his vision of national redemption in Palestine. Eliot, in turn, had the unhappy task of comforting him and even, on one occasion, dissuading him from suicide when he began to suffer from the cancer that eventually killed him. He was on his way to

Palestine in May 1873, but did not reach it, dying in Alexandria where he was buried in the Jewish cemetery. Eliot heard the news at the very time that she was planning *Daniel Deronda*, which may be taken, in a sense, as a memorial to him—to him personally in the guise of Mordecai, and to his vision of Judaism.

It is not known when Eliot made her famous pronouncement that God was "inconceivable," immortality "unbelievable," and Duty nonetheless "peremptory and absolute."[31] If *Middlemarch* may be read as a secular testament to the idea of Duty, her next and last novel, *Daniel Deronda*, represented something of a return to an Old Testament, with Faith in the service of Duty. For Deronda, Duty was still "peremptory and absolute," but God was no longer "inconceivable."

Eliot had *Daniel Deronda* in mind even before she completed *Middlemarch*. The first of her several notebooks on Jewish subjects dated from the summer of 1872. In September, when she and Lewes were at a spa in Germany, she viewed the scene at the gambling tables which inspired the opening chapter of *Daniel Deronda*. "The saddest thing to be witnessed," she wrote her publisher, "is the play of Miss Leigh, Byron's grand-niece, who is only 26 years old, and is completely in the grasp of this mean, money-making demon. It made me cry to see her young fresh face among the hags and brutally stupid men around her."[32] A year later she reported to her publisher, "I am slowly simmering towards another big book; but people seem so bent on giving supremacy to 'Middlemarch' that that they are sure not to like any future book so well."[33]

That "simmering," which had been going on for well over a year, consisted of a massive work of research into Jewish learning and lore. Eliot's notebooks for this period contained excerpts from the Bible and Prophets, the Mishnah and Talmud, Maimonides, medieval rabbis and Kabbalistic works, as well as contemporary German scholars (Moses Mendelssohn, Heinrich Graetz, Moritz Steinschneider, Leopold Zunz, Abraham Geiger, Abraham Berliner, Emanuel Deutsch), French scholars (Ernest Renan, Jassuda Bédarride, Georges Depping, Salomon Munk), English scholars (Henry Milman, Christian David Ginsburg, Abraham Benisch, David de Sola, Hyam Isaacs), and scores of others. Lady Strangford, Deutsch's friend and literary executor, made available to Eliot a copy of his *Literary Remains* which she was about to publish, as well as her own extensive knowledge of the Near East. (Her late husband, the Viscount Strangford, was said to have been the original of Disraeli's Coningsby.) Eliot borrowed books from the London Library, and her own library was considerable (Lewes was constantly on the lookout for books on Judaica for her), including works by the sages and scholars, as well as Hebrew dictionaries, lexicons, grammars, and prayer books.

Noting the thousands of excerpts in her notebooks, one is impressed by the self-restraint Eliot exercised in displaying this wealth of scholarship in *Daniel Deronda*. Only the tip of the iceberg appeared—in Deronda's purchase, for example, in a Jewish bookstore, of "that wonderful bit of autobiography, the life of the Polish Jew, Salomon Maimon."[34*] Or Mordecai's recital of a poem written (possibly by Eliot herself) in

---

* In her copy of this book, Eliot corrected some of Maimon's errors of fact and misinterpretations of the Kabbala.

imitation of the medieval Jewish poet, Jehuda Halevi.[35] Or the epigraph from Zunz, repeated in the opening sentence of the chapter, on Israel's unhappy primacy in the "ranks of suffering."[36] Another epigraph is a chilling quotation from the Mishnah (not identified as such): "No man may turn the bones of his father and mother into spoons," followed by Eliot's no less startling and prophetic commentary: "The market for spoons has never expanded enough for anyone to say, 'Why not?'"[37]

At one point, Mordecai compares his lot to that of Joshua ben Chananja who, after the destruction of the Temple, "earned his bread by making needles, but in his youth he had been a singer on the steps of the Temple, and had a memory of what was, before the glory departed."[38] Looking to Deronda as his disciple, Mordecai reflects upon the Kabbalistic doctrine of the rebirth of souls and of a second soul that would complement the first.[39] Deronda himself recalls the "Rabbi who stood waiting at the gate of Rome in confidence that the Messiah would be found among the destitute who entered there," an allusion, identified in the notebooks but not the novel, to another sage of a later generation.[40]

And then there are the more prosaic references in the novel to the everyday life of ordinary Jews. A Christian girl, accompanying Mirah, the young Jewish heroine, to the synagogue, asks whether it seems right to her that the women are seated behind rails in a gallery apart, and whether she likes to see the men wearing hats.[41] Mirah worries whether her brother is alive to say *Kaddish* in memory of their mother, and her brother, when they finally meet, explains to her the meaning of the *Shema*, "the chief devotional exercise of the Hebrew."[42] Deronda, inquiring about the time of service at a synagogue, is asked whether he wants "the fine new building

of the Reformed" or "the old Rabbinical school of the orthodox." Entering the "*Rabbinische Schule*," he notices the *tali-
thim* worn by the men, listens to the chant of the *Chazan*, and
observes the swaying of the men's bodies as they pray.[43] A
Sabbath dinner with the Cohens introduces him to the rituals
of the occasion: the benediction of the children by the father,
the washing of his hands before the meal, the distribution
of pieces of the bread to the family, all accompanied by the
appropriate Hebrew prayers.[44]

It is also interesting to be introduced, early in the novel, to
a figure who was to play an important part in the lives of both
the Jewish and non-Jewish characters, thus linking both parts
of the novel. The Jewish musician Herr Klesmer, "a felicitous
combination of the German, the Sclave, and the Semite," was
clearly modeled on Anton Rubinstein (his mother a German
Jew, his father Russian), whom Eliot and Lewes had met in
Weimar in 1854 and again in London in 1876. More interesting is the name Eliot gives him in the novel. *Klezmer* is
the Yiddish word originally referring to the musical instru-
ments used in the playing of Ashkenazi folk music and, later,
by extension, applied to the Jewish musicians themselves.[45]
(Today it describes the genre of music familiar at Jewish wed-
dings and other celebratory occasions.)

It was an arduous initiation George Eliot went through in
preparation for *Daniel Deronda*, a rigorous course of self-
education in a tradition and a culture remote from her own.
Yet perhaps not so remote, for even as she immersed herself in
Judaic studies, she was also reading and researching secular
subjects, comfortably moving from one to the other. A set

of notebooks on Judaica, for example, opened with a section on Homeric studies, quoting modern scholars as well as the ancients—Pindar, Herodotus, Thucydides, Aristophanes, Xenophon (many quoted in Greek)—on such controverted matters as the authorship, dating, and meaning of the *Iliad* and *Odyssey*. This was followed by another briefer section on science, citing John Tyndall on light, James Clerk Maxwell on molecules, and Comte on geometry. Only then did the notebooks turn to the Mishnah, Talmud, and other Jewish sources, but even these were interrupted by excerpts from the satires of Persius (quoted in Latin). Similarly, an account of the "Jewish Year" (the Jewish calendar, with a list of the feasts and fasts) was followed by Comte's Positivist Calendar, with its heroes and festivals.

An earlier notebook contained a list of her readings from September 1872 to June 1873, the "simmering" period for *Daniel Deronda*:

Freitag on Dramatic Art
Kompert's Stories of the Ghetto
Tracts on Science in Virchow & Holzendorff's Series
Geiger on the Aryans
Wilkinson's Ancient Egyptians
Articles on Egypt in Geographical & Biblical Dictionaries
Burnouf's Science des Religions (aloud)
Herodotus Book II. On Egypt
Morte d'Arthur
Romans de la Table Ronde
Freeman's Old English History
Tristram Shandy (aloud)
Schopenhauer's Welt als Wille u. Vorstelling
Keat's Hyperion and Minor Poems

Fawcett's Political Economy
Portions of Mill's ditto
Comte's Catechism—2d and 3d Parts
Aeneid, B.VI
Odyssey B. XI
Fragments of Sappho. Mimnermus, Frag.
Marx's Life of Beethoven
Buckle's Hist. of Civil. (aloud)
Phaedrus
Iliad B. XVIII and XIX
Phaedo
Maine's Village Communities [46]

This list somehow omitted another book. In May 1873, Eliot noted in her journal, "I am just finishing again Aristotle's 'Poetics,' which I first read in 1856."[47] A quotation from the "Poetics" was an epigraph to one of the chapters in *Daniel Deronda*: "It is a part of probability that many improbable things will happen."[48] That epigraph was an appropriate introduction to the section of the novel entitled "Revelations," in which many improbable things did, indeed, happen.

Victorians writers seem to have had an enormous capacity for reading as well as writing (books, essays, reviews, and voluminous letters), all of this while travelling incessantly, often under difficult conditions, and nurturing varieties of ailments, some of which were nearly incapacitating. Eliot was more than their equal. Even if one partially discounts that list of books read in less than a year, even if she only skimmed or "read in" some of them, it is impressive as evidence of an extraordinary breadth of interests and knowledge.

As the prelude to *Daniel Deronda*, it is all the more interesting, for it suggests that, whatever critics may have thought about the alien and extraneous "Jewish element" in the novel, she herself did not think of Judaism as an alien or extraneous element in Western civilization. She read the Jewish sources, ancient and modern, in the same appreciative spirit that she read the classics and literature of her own culture. And she placed them both in the same cultural continuum. This may have been her purpose in introducing the chapters with epigraphs ranging from the Old Testament to Aristotle, Marcus Aurelius, Molière, Montaigne, Dante, Fontenelle, La Rochefoucauld, Heine, Zunz, and such English worthies as Shakespeare, Milton, Spenser, Sterne, Coleridge, Shelley, Keats, Wordsworth. The effect was to place the Jewish theme, which might seem sectarian or parochial, in the largest cultural and cosmopolitan context. The epigraph from Aristotle's "Poetics," for example, was preceded by one from Wordsworth's "Excursion" and was followed by another from Zunz's *Die Synagogale Poesie des Mittelalters*.

To those critics who wanted to separate the Jewish element of the novel from the English, Eliot protested that it was all of a whole. So, too, Judaism, for her, although unique in its faith, its people, and its history, was of a whole with the culture and history of mankind. This is one of the lessons of *Daniel Deronda*. And this is why Deronda the disciple, not Mordecai the prophet, is the eponymous hero of the novel. Deronda embodies the wholeness of Judaism, retaining the virtues of the English Christian gentleman, as he once was, while discovering and abiding by his true faith as a Jew—and, more dramatically, fulfilling his mission as a pioneer in the Jewish homeland in Palestine.

III.

DANIEL DERONDA'S
INITIATION *and*
REVELATION

In January 1874, Eliot started what she described as "Sketches towards Daniel Deronda."[1] By May of the following year she had written the first part, by October the second. She had not completed the book when it began to appear in monthly installments from February to September 1876.

The opening scene recalls the gambling episode Eliot had witnessed a few years earlier. (That too had been at a German resort.) The scene is introduced with a series of tantalizing questions:

> Was she beautiful or not beautiful? and what was the
> secret of form or expression which gave the dynamic qual-
> ity to her glance? Was the good or the evil genius domi-
> nant in those beams? Probably the evil; else why was the
> effect that of unrest rather than of undisturbed charm?
> Why was the wish to look again felt as coercion and not
> as a longing in which the whole being consents?[2]

These first sentences (they might have been written by Henry James) capture the ambiguous nature of the two leading characters and their relationship—the young woman, Gwendolen Harleth, who is gambling and the young man, Daniel Deronda, who is watching her, not longingly or lovingly but almost obsessively. She has been winning until she meets his gaze and, as if it had been "an evil eye," begins to lose, staking everything and losing everything. Later that evening, expressing curiosity about the man who had been observing her, she is told that he is an Englishman, a Mr. Deronda, a relative of Sir Hugo Mallinger, who happens to live near her. Her informant can not tell her more about Deronda because he had not said anything when they had met; indeed he looked bored. Gwendolen is all the more eager to meet him, because she too is always bored. That is why she gambled. "Bored to death," she explains, she has to "make something happen," go to Switzerland, perhaps, and "up the Matterhorn." Perhaps, her friend suggests, Mr. Deronda's acquaintance would do instead of the Matterhorn. "Perhaps," she replies.[3]

Gwendolen does not meet Deronda then. Nor does she the following day, when a letter from her mother summons her home with the news that her family suddenly finds itself impoverished. Deciding upon a last fling at the roulette table, she pawns her necklace, complaining about "these Jew dealers [who] were so unscrupulous in taking advantage of Christians unfortunate at play." Upon her return to her hotel, she finds a packet at her door containing the necklace she has just pawned with a note from "a stranger" who found it and hoped she would not again risk losing it. Humiliated and angry, she departs immediately for home, without reappearing at the gambling table.[4]

The chapter describing her return opens ominously: "Pity that Offendene was not the home of Miss Harleth's childhood, or endeared to her by family memories!" Offendene has been the family home for only a year since her step-father's death. Before that, she and her mother (widowed, remarried, and now widowed again) and four half-sisters had been living abroad, roving from one watering-place to another. Now, with the family's impoverishment, they are going to move yet again, from the spacious house where she was beginning to feel at home to a cottage with only two small parlors and four bedrooms. The passage following that cryptic remark about Offendene might serve as the epigraph to the novel as a whole.

> A human life, I think, should be well rooted in some spot of a native land, where it may get the love of tender kinship for the face of earth, for the labours men go forth to, for the sounds and accents that haunt it, for whatever will give that early home a familiar unmistakable difference amidst the future widening of knowledge: a spot where the definitiveness of early memories may be inwrought with affection, and kindly acquaintance with all neighbours, even to the dogs and donkeys, may spread not by sentimental effort and reflection, but as a sweet habit of blood. . . . The best introduction to astronomy is to think of the nightly heavens as a little lot of stars belonging to one's own homestead.[5]

This is the underlying motif of the novel: the quest for identity—the identities, most obviously, of Deronda and Mirah searching for their parents and heritage, but also

Gwendolen searching for her true self. Lacking the roots, memories, and "sweet habit of blood" that come with one's own homestead, she seeks an identity independent of kin and kind. Like a latter-day feminist, she is a free spirit trying to "find herself," cherishing her individuality and autonomy, resenting and resisting everything and everyone that might impinge upon her freedom. This is to be her fatal weakness: a narcissism that comes from a spurious sense of identity, a self that is entirely self-contained, self-fashioned, self-willed—and, ultimately, self-destructive.

This "spoiled child" (as the title of the first book describes her) occupies center stage for the first hundred pages of the novel. The poverty which has suddenly befallen her family threatens to condemn her either to the humiliating job of governess or, more suitably, to marriage. She has always assumed that one day she must be married, but she does not look forward to it. "She meant to do what was pleasant to herself in a striking manner; or rather, whatever she could do so as to strike others with admiration and get in that reflected way a more ardent sense of living."[6] Marriage, even a good marriage, will not satisfy her. Indeed, the idea repels her. Rex, the rector's son, a good-natured young man, is in love with her and eager to marry her. She does not mind passing the time with him and is pleased with the "small romance" of his devotion, but the idea of anything more is repugnant. She feels "a sort of physical repulsion to being directly made love to. . . . There was a certain fierceness of maidenhood in her." When he actually declares his love and tries to take her hand, she recoils from him. "Pray don't make love to me! I hate it," she says, looking at him fiercely. "I shall never love anybody," she tells her mother. "I can't love people. I hate them."[7]

Yet she does entertain the prospect of marriage with another suitor, Mallinger Grandcourt (Sir Hugo's nephew). She is not in love with him, but she is attracted to "the dignities, the luxuries, the power of doing a great deal of what she liked to do," which that marriage would provide. And she would marry him on her terms. She would "do just as she liked." She would not renounce her freedom, or "do as other women did," certainly not come under the "subjection" of a husband. After marriage, she is confident, she would be able to "manage him thoroughly."[8]

So far, Gwendolen is merely a spoiled child, subject to the all too familiar temptations of a good (that is, expedient) marriage—doing, in fact, "as other women did." The test of her character comes when a truly venomous character, Mr. Lush, the factotum to Grandcourt, arranges for her to meet in secret Grandcourt's long-time mistress and the mother of his two children. Mrs. Glasher begs her not to marry Grandcourt, for that will deprive her son of his rightful inheritance. Gwendolen, feeling a "sort of terror," an inner "revulsion," promises only not to tell Grandcourt that they have met.[9] Returning home, she informs her mother that she will not marry Grandcourt. Eventually, however, confronted with the reality of poverty and the dire prospect of becoming a governess, and half-pretending to herself that she is marrying for the sake of her family, she agrees to the marriage. After the engagement, lying in bed with wide-open eyes, "looking on darkness which the blind do see" (the quotation from Shakespeare makes the scene all the more portentous), she is appalled to realize that she is about to do what has been so repugnant to her. "It was new to her that a question of right or wrong in her conduct should rouse her to terror."[10]

In marrying Grandcourt, Gwendolen becomes complicitous in his immorality, condoning his behavior, in effect, because she is aware of it and marries him nevertheless. She suffers the further ignominy of knowing that he knows that she knows of it. Grandcourt, for his part, marries her not because he loves her but because she was a challenge to him. While she thinks she can "manage" him, he is intent upon demonstrating his "mastery" of her, which is all the more satisfying for him because of her abject surrender.[11] The marriage is, inevitably, an unmitigated tragedy. She who so yearned for freedom is the slave, he the master. She is finally released from his tyranny when he accidentally drowns. But even then she is not truly liberated because she bears the moral guilt of his death. She might not have been able to save him, but she knows that she made no effort to do so. And she has to live with that guilty knowledge.*

Deronda does not play an active part in this stage of the drama, but his shadow, and sometimes his presence, hovers over it. He is Gwendolen's conscience and father confessor—and, as she sees it, her unrequited lover. Before, during, and after her marriage, she repeatedly appeals to him for advice and support. And on the morning of his wedding day, as if to

---

* There is more than a hint of lesbianism in Gwendolen's aversion to marriage. If the very declaration of love by Rex provoked so "fierce" a physical repulsion, the act of love, sexual intercourse, would surely have been even more repellent. The only explanation offered for her childless marriage is her dread of becoming a mother because it would be a living testimony of her guilt in marrying him. One scene suggests something like a rape—rape in the guise of a kiss. Knowing that Gwendolen was in a "desperate rage" with him, Grandcourt deliberately "turned her chin and kissed her, while she still kept her eyelids down, and she did not move them until he was on the other side of the door."[12] Their marriage is almost a case-study of the radical-feminist view of marriage as a sexual predation and bondage.

release him from any culpability he may feel in not returning her love, she sends him a letter that is more precious to him than any wedding present:

> Do not think of me sorrowfully on your wedding-day. I have remembered your words—that I may live to be one of the best of women, who make others glad that they were born. I do not yet see how that can be, but you know better than I. If it ever comes, it will be because you helped me. I only thought of myself, and I made you grieve. It hurts me now to think of your grief. You must not grieve any more for me. It is better—it shall be better with me because I have known you.[13]

In the novel, the Gwendolen story, up to the time of her engagement, appears first. Chronologically, however, Deronda's story precedes it. A few months before he went abroad and witnessed that scene at the gambling table, he had the more memorable experience of rescuing a young woman who was about to drown herself.* Rowing on the Thames one summer evening, singing to himself an aria from a favorite opera, he sees a woman on the bank clearly intent upon suicide. Her first endearing words to him, as he draws her from the water, are to identify the song he was singing. She then explains that she had been brought to her desperate strait by her vain search for her long-lost mother and brother. "I am English

---

* The parallel between the two drownings—Mirah saved from drowning by Deronda, and Gwendolen saved, in another sense, by her husband's drowning—has the effect of binding together the two "parts" of the novel.

born. But I am a Jewess," she tells him when he remarks upon her foreign accent.[14] She hopes he will not despise her; she knows that many Jews are bad. But so, too, Deronda retorts, are many Christians, and he hopes she will not despise him for that. Moved by her tale (and by her beauty), Deronda takes her to the home of his generous friends, the Meyricks, who welcome the "young Jewess" and insist that she live with them until she finds her relatives.

Mirah Lapidoth tells them her story. She was seven when her father spirited her away from her mother and took her to live with him, first in New York and then in Hamburg, Vienna, Prague, or wherever his trade took him. He was an actor and stage-manager, and he trained her to be a singer, which she disliked as a profession although she enjoyed music and singing. She fled from Prague when her father, imprisoned for some reason not known to her, sent her to see a count who would arrange for her father's release on condition, she realized, that she become his lover. She came to England to seek her mother and her brother Ezra, knowing little about them except their name, which is Cohen. (Her father, preferring not to be known as Jewish, had changed his name, and hers, to Lapidoth.) Although she has little knowledge of Judaism, she has strong sentimental attachments to it, remembering her mother singing Hebrew hymns to her.

Mirah's tale is all the more moving for Deronda because he too is haunted by the thought of a missing mother—and a father as well. Although Sir Hugo represents himself as his guardian, Deronda suspects that he is his natural father. About his mother he knows nothing, but, hearing Mirah's story, he is reminded of the "dread' he himself feels about his own mother, and he is tempted to warn her that her happy childhood memories might be illusory, that her mother might turn out to be not at all what she imagines. Nevertheless, he promises to help her in her search, while she remains the guest of the hospitable Meyricks.

What makes Mirah especially intriguing, for Deronda as for the Meyricks, is the fact that she is proud to be Jewish. Until that time, Deronda, although he had a "strong tendency to side with the objects of prejudice," knew little about Jews and was not much interested in them. "The facts he knew about them, whether they walked conspicuous in fine apparel or lurked in by-streets, were chiefly of the sort most repugnant to him. Of learned and accomplished Jews, he took it for granted that they had dropped their religion, and wished to be merged in the people of their native lands." For the rest, he simply assumed that Jews had "the virtues and vices of a long-oppressed race."[15] Like his countrymen, he regarded Judaism "as a sort of eccentric fossilised form" of interest only to scholars. Mirah makes him aware not only of Jews as existing, actual persons but of Judaism itself as a living reality. Fleeing from one parent and yearning after the other, she had impressed upon him "the hitherto neglected reality that Judaism was something still throbbing in human lives."[16]

Wandering around London, looking at synagogues and exploring Jewish bookstores (it is in one of these that he comes across the autobiography of Salomon Maimon), and on the alert for the names of Mirah's mother and brother, Deronda comes upon a pawnshop with the name "Ezra Cohen" over the shop window. Returning later on the pretext of pawning a ring, on a Friday evening after the shop is closed for the Sabbath, he is admitted to the family's quarters and invited to share the Sabbath meal with them. He is startled to see

another man at the table, the strange man from the bookstore who had sold him the Maimon book and had inquired
whether Deronda was "of our race."[17]

This is Mordecai, who is to initiate Deronda into Judaism.
Mordecai is clearly of the same race as the Cohens, Deronda
realizes, but of a quite different breed. Where the Cohens are
placid and commonplace, good-natured but somewhat vulgar
(Deronda is distressed to think that this might be Mirah's long-
lost family), Mordecai is learned and passionately committed to Judaism. He is also emaciated and sickly, aged beyond
his years (he is only thirty), and impoverished, living with the
Cohens in return for his help in repairing jewelry in their shop
and earning a pittance as a part-time worker in the bookstore.
Just as Mordecai, in that brief encounter in the bookstore, suspects Deronda of being "of our race," so Deronda sees in him
the "physiognomy" that might have been that of "a prophet of
the Exile" or a "New Hebrew poet of the mediaeval time."[18]

In a dramatic scene suggesting a laying-on-of-hands,
Mordecai, sensing his imminent death, appeals to Deronda
as a kindred spirit, a disciple to whom he can transmit his
feelings and beliefs and who will carry out his mission. Such a
man, Mordecai specifies, would have to be a Jew, "intellectu-
ally cultured, morally fervid," but, unlike himself, physically
"beautiful and strong."[19] In Deronda, in spite of his protes-
tations that he is not Jewish, Mordecai thinks he has found
that person. To make Deronda understand what he is asking
of him, he recounts his own spiritual odyssey. He is a Jew

born in England: "English is my mother tongue, England is the native land of this body." But in his youth, he had gone abroad to study, first in Holland, with his uncle, a Rabbi, and then in Hamburg and Göttingen, where he acquired a larger knowledge of the Gentile as well as the Jewish world, and where he truly came to understand and appreciate his Jewishness. "Then ideas, beloved ideas, came to me because I was a Jew. They were a trust to fulfil, because I was a Jew. They were an inspiration, because I was a Jew, and felt the heart of my race beating within me. They were my life; I was not fully born till then."[20]

Assured by Deronda that his own experience has given him a keen interest in "a spiritual destiny embraced willingly, and embraced in youth," Mordecai corrects him. His destiny was not embraced in youth; it came from within, bringing with it its own world, a mediaeval world, where men made the ancient language live again in "new psalms of exile." They were men who had absorbed "the philosophy of the Gentile into the faith of the Jew, and they still yearned toward a centre for our race." One of their souls had entered into him, bringing with it the memories of their world. That soul had "travelled into Spain and Provence; it debated with Aben-Ezra; it took ship with Jehuda ha-Levi; it heard the roar of the Crusaders and the shrieks of tortured Israel." It spoke the language they had made alive, and could only speak in that language, so long as that soul was imprisoned within him. Mordecai has tried to talk to men of his own faith, but scholar and merchant alike are deaf to him or too busy to listen. They see only a poor sick man clutching a bundle of Hebrew manuscripts.[21]

"I feel with you—I feel strongly with you," Deronda tells him, and promises to see to the publication of his writings. That is not enough, Mordecai replies.

> You must be not only a hand to me, but a soul—believing my belief—being moved by my reasons—hoping my hope—seeing the vision I point to—beholding a glory where I behold it! . . . You will be my life: it will be planted afresh; it will grow. You shall take the inheritance; it has been gathering for ages. The generations are crowding on my narrow life as a bridge: what has been and what is to be are meeting there; and the bridge is breaking. But I have found you. You have come in time. You will take the inheritance which the base son refuses . . . : you will take the sacred inheritance of the Jew.[22]

Deronda becomes as pale as Moredecai. He does not want to hurt this suffering creature but neither does he want to feed his illusion. Tenderly, he takes Mordecai's hand and reminds him what he told him earlier, that he is not of his race. "It can't be true," Mordecai protests. "You are not sure of your own origin." How does he know that? Deronda asks. "I know it—I know it," Mordecai replies, "what is my life else?" Only then does Deronda tell him about his own questionable origin. He has never known his mother and knows nothing about her, and he has never called any man father but is convinced that his father is an Englishman. "You *shall* know." Mordecai assures him. "What are we met for but that you should know?" They part, Deronda much moved but also troubled by the commitment Mordecai is asking of him.[23]

Reflecting later upon Mordecai's demand of discipleship, Deronda sees how visionary it is, but he also realizes that that is not itself reason to dismiss it out of hand. He is even prepared to admit that he might come to share some of Mordecai's ideas, even entertain the bare possibility that he is Jewish—only the bare possibility, for he is still convinced that Sir Hugo is his father. Meeting Mordecai again at the Cohens, he is conscious of how different they are from their lodger. He is reminded of a passage he has read in Leopold Zunz's book: "If there are ranks in suffering, Israel takes precedence of all the nations—if the duration of sorrows and the patience with which they are borne ennoble, the Jews are among the aristocracy of every land." The Cohens do not have that mark of aristocracy. The pawnbroker is not a symbol of the great Jewish epic. Yet perhaps it is typical, Deronda reflects, that a person like Mordecai, "a frail incorporation of the national consciousness, breathing with difficult breath—was nested in the self-congratulating ignorant prosperity of the Cohens." Mordecai himself has a more generous view of his hosts, and not only because they have been good to him: "They have the heart of the Israelite within them," he reminds Deronda, "though they are as the horse and the mule, without understanding beyond the narrow path they tread."[24]

It is among his friends, not all Jews, that Mordecai proves to be a considerable intellectual and controversialist, as well as a man of vision and passion. He invites Deronda to a meeting of his club, "The Philosophers," he calls it ironically, at the Hand and Banner pub. It consists of a group of poor workingmen (a bookseller, a saddler, a watchmaker, a shoemaker, and the like), three of them Jewish, all with a taste for ideas and spirited discussion.* The subject for the evening is "the law of progress," which soon devolves into a debate about nationality and, more specifically, Jewish nationality. To the argument put forward by one of the Jews, that progress means the death of both the idea and the sentiment of nationality, Deronda (in one of his few interventions) replies that the sentiment might yet revive, as nations revive. We might even live, he predicts, to see "a great outburst of force in the Arabs, who are being inspired with a new zeal."† Mordecai agrees. If there is a tendency against nationality, it should be resisted. "The life of a people grows, it is knit together and yet expanded, in joy and sorrow, in thought and action." Gideon, representing himself as a "rational Jew," explains that he regards his people as a family, approves of their worship "in a rational way," and sees no reason for their conversion to Christianity now that they have political equality. But he is also for ridding themselves of their superstitions and of their "exclusiveness." "There's no reason now why we shouldn't melt grad-

---

* Lewes had belonged to just such a club when he was a young man. In an article on Spinoza in the *Fortnightly Review* in 1866, he was reminded of that club because it was there that he was introduced to Spinoza, to whom he immediately felt an affinity and was moved to translate the *Ethics*. (It was Eliot who later did that translation.) Like Mordecai's club, Lewes's included the keeper of a second-hand bookstall, a watchmaker, and a bootmaker. One of the contemporary reviewers of *Daniel Deronda* suggested that Cohn, the consumptive watch-maker in Lewes' club, was the model for Mordecai, but both Eliot and Lewes denied this. Cohn, Lewes said, had no "specifically Jewish enthusiasm," and Eliot pointed out that Cohn was of the "Spinoza type," in contrast to Mordecai.[25]
† "Arab" was commonly used to mean "semite," including Jews as well as Muslims and Christians."

ually into the populations we live among. That's the order of the day in point of progress. I would as soon my children married Christians as Jews. And I'm for the old maxim, 'A man's country is where he's well off.'"[26]

Mordecai, too, claims to be a "rational Jew":

But what is it to be rational—what is it to feel the light
of the divine reason growing stronger within and without? It is to see more and more of the hidden bonds that
bind and consecrate change as a dependent growth—yea,
consecrate it with kinship: the past becomes my parent,
and the future stretches towards me the appealing arms
of children. . . . Each nation has its own work, and is a
member of the world, enriched by the work of each. But it
is true, as Jehuda ha-Levi first said, that Israel is the heart
of mankind, if we mean by heart the core of affection
which binds a race and its families in dutiful love, and
the reverence for the human body which lifts the needs of
our animal life into religion, and the tenderness which is
merciful to the poor and weak and to the dumb creature
that wears the yoke for us.[27]

A non-Jew protests. Whatever the Jews once contributed, they are now an arrogant people, stubbornly adherent to the "superannuated." They show their abilities well enough when they take up liberal ideas, "but as a race they have no development in them." Mordecai denies these charges. The Jewish people are not superannuated; the soul of Judaism is not dead; and they can look forward to the future, the resto-ration of Israel as "a land and a polity." "Revive the organic centre: let the unity of Israel . . . be an outward reality. Look-ing towards a land and a polity, our dispersed people in all the ends of the earth may share the dignity of a national life which has a voice among the people of the East and the West." To those who object that Palestine has become the haven of the "raff and scum" of Jews, poor Jews who went there to be maintained like able-bodied paupers, Mordecai offers a different vision of Palestine:

> I say that the effect of our separateness will not be completed and have its highest transformation unless our race takes on again the character of a nationality. . . . There is a store of wisdom among us to found a new Jewish polity, grand, simple, just, like the old—a republic where there is equality of protection. . . . The outraged Jew shall have a defence in the court of nations, as the outraged Englishman or American. And the world will gain as Israel gains. For there will be a community in the van of the East which carries the culture and the sympathies of every great nation in its bosom.[28]

Mordecai has the last word in the debate. "Let us . . . claim the brotherhood of our nation, and carry into it a new brotherhood with the nations of the Gentiles. The vision is there; it will be fulfilled." The group disperses, sensing that nothing more can be said. After recovering from his impassioned talk, Mordecai turns to Deronda and appeals to him once again, citing a doctrine of the Kabbala about the rebirth of old tired souls, perfected and purified, in new bodies: "When my long-wandering soul is liberated from this weary body, it will join yours, and its work will be perfected."[29]

The unexpected sequel to this episode is the revelation of Mirah's identity. Recalling a moment years ago when he was about to make his journey to the East, Mordecai casually remarks that his companion, bringing him a letter, had addressed him as Ezra. To the astonished Deronda, he explains that the letter was from his mother who always called him Ezra. She has long since died, grieving for her daughter Mirah who had been taken from her by her husband, just as Mordecai himself is grieving for his lost sister. He later tells Deronda that his full name is Ezra Mordecai Cohen—not related to the Cohens with whom he has been lodging, except for their common kinship in Israel. Thus the identity quest of Mirah is resolved. Mirah can say the prayer for the dead in memory of her mother and can finally meet her long-lost brother Ezra. (They also later meet their father, whom they try to help but who is as manipulative and unscrupulous as ever, stealing Deronda's ring before disappearing from their lives.)

That leaves the primary mystery of Deronda's identity. And that is solved when Sir Hugo explains that he has kept Deronda's parentage secret on the request of his mother, whose health is now failing and who has expressed a desire to see her son. Deronda's father, Sir Hugo adds, is no longer alive, thus disposing of Deronda's illusion about Sir Hugo himself. His mother's letter to Deronda suggesting that they meet is formally signed "Your unknown mother, Leonora Halm-Eberstein." (As a result of a second marriage to a Russian noble, she is Princess Halm-Eberstein.)

The meeting of mother and son, in Genoa where she lives and is now dying, is as dramatic as the laying-on-of-hands scene with Mordecai. In a sense, it is a sequel to that scene, for Deronda now learns that his mother is Jewish, thus qualifying him as Mordecai's disciple. It is also here that the Gwendolen and Deronda themes merge again, if only implicitly. Gwendolen's name is never mentioned, but her figure hovers over his mother's story, some of their complaints and desires being uncannily similar—his mother, however, succeeding where Gwendolen so tragically failed. His mother, like Gwendolen, aspired to be a liberated woman, resenting the restrictions and demands made upon her by her father. Again like Gwendolen, she did not want to marry but was forced to do so by her father. She acquiesced in that marriage, as Gwendolen had, because she believed she could "rule" her husband. "I had a right to be free. I had a right to seek my freedom from a bondage that I hated."[30] Unlike Gwendolen, however, her marriage provided her with that freedom. Her husband (in dramatic contrast to Grandcourt) was enamored of her, sacrificing his own business (banking and money-changing) to enable her to pursue her career as a singer and an actress.

Having sought and found her freedom in marriage, when her husband died she sought and found it again, by giving up her two-year-old child to an old friend, Sir Hugo, who was in love with her and who promised to raise the boy as "an English gentleman." "I had not much affection to give you," she tells Deronda. "I did not want affection. I had been stifled with it. I wanted to live out the life that was in me, and not to be hampered with other lives." She does not feel about children "as other women feel" (again, echoing Gwendolen, who was not going to do "as other women did"). "I was glad to be freed from you," she tells him, with the merciless frankness and honesty that she brings to the whole of their conversation.[31]

But it was not only freedom from the conventional role of wife and mother that she sought. It was also freedom from the religion of her father, from the "bondage" of Judaism. In giving up her son she was giving him the freedom she sought for herself. "The bondage I hated for myself I wanted to keep you from. What better could the most loving mother have done? I relieved you from the bondage of having been born a Jew." She is surprised by Deronda's reception to this news. "Then I *am* a Jew? My father was a Jew, and you are a Jewess?" Yes, his father was her cousin. "I am glad of it," he exclaims. She cannot understand this. He is now "an English gentleman," she points out; she has secured that for him. When he objects to her having chosen his "birthright" for him, she tells him that she chose for him what she would have chosen for herself. "How could I know that you would have the spirit of my father in you? How could I know that you would love what I hated?—if you really love to be a Jew."[32]

The Judaism her father wanted to impose upon her was onerous to her because it was irrational as well as restrictive.

> I was to feel awe for the bit of parchment in the *mezuza*
> over the door; to dread lest a bit of butter should touch a
> bit of meat; to think it beautiful that men should bind the
> *tephillin* on them, and women not, —to adore the wisdom
> of such laws, however silly they might seem to me. . . . I
> was to care for ever about what Israel had been; and I did
> not care at all. I cared for the wide world, and all that I
> could represent in it. . . . I wanted to live a large life, with
> freedom to do what every one else did, and be carried
> along in a great current, not obliged to care. . . . You are
> glad to have been born a Jew. You say so. That is because
> you have not been brought up as a Jew. That separateness
> seems sweet to you because I saved you from it.[33]

Hers was a double bondage: being a Jew, and, worse yet, a Jewish woman with ambition and talent. "You can never imagine what it is to have a man's force of genius in you, and yet to suffer the slavery of being a girl. To have a pattern cut out—'this is the Jewish woman; this is what you must be.'" Her father had wanted a son; she was a makeshift substitute. He especially hated Jewish women appearing before the Christian world as singers and actresses, which was what she did, and did very well, to the envy of others. Her husband, fortunately, was very different from her father—and different, too, from herself. Unlike her, he was "all lovingness and affection." He was willing to be ruled by her and put no hindrance in the way of her career. Her father, a learned man, a clever physician, and a good man, was also a man with an iron will, whose "heart was set on his Judaism." "Such men turn their wives and daughters into slaves. They would rule the world if they could, but not ruling the world, they throw all the weight of their will on the necks and souls of women."[34]

Nature, however, sometimes thwarted even the most determined of men. Her father's only child was a girl, a girl, moreover, as strong-minded as he was. Some of that strength of will came from her mother's family. Her mother, an English Jew of Portuguese descent whom her father had married in England, had died when her daughter was eight.* The girl was brought up by her mother's sister, a singer married to an Englishman in Genoa, who saw to it that her niece was

---

* This heritage gave Deronda a legitimate claim to be an "English gentleman" as well as a good Jew—a Sephardi Jew, moreover. Later, revealing the discovery of his Jewishness to Mordecai, Daniel proudly informed him that he was not only a Jew but of "a line of Spanish Jews that has borne many students and men of practical power."[35]

taught music and encouraged her to become a professional singer, much to the dismay of her father. Disappointed in his daughter, her father looked for a grandson who would be a Jew like himself. Deronda's mother was determined that that would not happen, which was why she put him in the care of a good Englishman who was not a Jew. "You were my son, and it was my turn to say what you should be. I said you should not know you were a Jew."[36]

Deronda is much moved by his mother's recital, feeling a great affection for her even as she professes to feel little for him, but also resentful that she has kept his parentage and, more, his Jewishness from him. He would have welcomed the news that he is Jewish. "I have always been rebelling against the secrecy that looked like shame. It is no shame to have Jewish parents—the shame is to disown it." But there is no reason to be ashamed, his mother insists: "I rid myself of the Jewish tatters and gibberish that make people nudge each other at sight of us. . . . I delivered you from the pelting contempt that pursues Jewish separateness. I am not ashamed that I did it. It was the better for you." She herself has not repented and has not changed her views. She remarried after nine years of freedom and professional success only because she was losing her voice and could not endure the prospect of decline. She was then baptized in order to be like the people she lived among. "I was not like a brute, obliged to go with my own herd." It was her "nature to resist" and she had a "right to resist."[37]

Now, with her strength gone, his mother feels the force of another "right," the bequest given her by her father for his grandson, a chest of old manuscripts and family papers. She had been tempted to burn it but was prevailed upon by her father's friend, Joseph Kalonymos, to give it to him in keeping for a future grandson. (She had told him that her son had died.) Years later, Kalonymos happened to meet Deronda in a Frankfurt synagogue, recognized the name, and berated her for pretending her son was dead and keeping his inheritance from him. She is now fulfilling that obligation by giving Deronda a letter by Kalonymos authorizing a bank in Mainz to return the chest to its rightful owner. She has also assigned the whole of his father's fortune to him, in a trust held by Sir Hugo. She may have deprived Deronda of the knowledge of his parentage and religion, but not, she assured him, of his fortune. "They can never accuse me of robbery there." [38]

Almost in passing, Deronda discovers that he has also been deprived of his real name. "Deronda" is the name of a distant branch of her husband's family, which she had given him to conceal his identity when she turned him over to Sir Hugo. When Deronda protests that this is yet another deception, his mother casually dismisses it. One name, she tells him, is "as real as another." "The Jews have always been changing their names." [39] His real name, Deronda now learns—that of his father and of his maternal grandfather as well (his parents were cousins)—is Charisi; his mother's professional name was Alcharisi. Forgiving her even this deception, Deronda offers to remain with her and comfort her. No, she replies, she has a husband and five children who do not know of his existence. She regrets that marriage too, but it is too late to undo it. On this note, tired but relieved to have carried out her father's bequest, she asks Deronda to leave, perhaps to come again soon.

A second meeting finds his mother in a more tender but still unrepentant mood. Would Deronda become the kind of Jew her father was, she wants to know?. No, he assures her, his education and "Christian sympathies" will prevent that, but he will identify himself with his people and do what he can for them. She sees the irony of this turn of events. In spite of herself, she has been the instrument of her father's will; she has given him a grandson with "a true Jewish heart." "Every Jew," he had said, "should rear his family as if he hoped that a Deliverer might spring from it." Deronda, hearing the echo of Mordecai in that sentiment, asks whether these were his exact words. Yes, she says, he had actually written them. As for her, she hopes her son can forgive her, and if he wants to say *Kaddish* for her, he should do so. "You will come between me and the dead."[40]

She has one final thought. Suspecting that Deronda is in love with a Jewess, she wants to know whether that is why he is glad to be a Jew (not for that reason alone, he tells her), whether she is beautiful (yes), and whether she is ambitious, having "a path of her own" (no, that is not her nature). Disappointed with the last answer, she nevertheless gives Deronda a jeweled miniature of her picture to be given to this woman who is so unlike herself. When Deronda suggests that surely she loves her children from her second marriage, she replies that she does, quickly adding, however: "I am not a loving woman. That is the truth. It is a talent to love—I lacked it. . . . I know very well what love makes of men and women—it is subjection. . . . I was never willingly subject to any man. Men have been subject to me."[41] The last meeting of mother and son (she is on her deathbed) ends with a kiss, but not before she reaffirms her own nature and beliefs.

When, shortly afterwards, Deronda goes to Mainz to pick up the chest, he meets Kalonymos and learns more about the grandfather who bequeathed it to him. Daniel Charisi, he is told, was a learned and cosmopolitan man. "He mingled all sorts of learning; and in that he was like our Arabic writers in the golden time." But he also remained a firm and faithful Jew: "What he used to insist on was that the strength and wealth of mankind depended on the balance of separateness and communication, and he was bitterly against our people losing themselves among the Gentiles." What, Kalonymos bluntly asks, is Daniel's vocation? Deronda confesses that he has no vocation. "Get one, get one. The Jew must be diligent." Would Deronda call himself a Jew and profess the faith of his fathers? He will call himself a Jew, Deronda answers, but not exactly as his fathers had. Indeed they themselves changed their horizons as they learned more about other "races." "But I think," Deronda assures him, "I can maintain my grandfather's notion of separateness with communication. I hold that my first duty is to my own people, and if there is anything to be done towards restoring or perfecting their common life, I shall make that my vocation." They then part, Deronda with his precious chest, and Kalonymos satisfied that he is, indeed, Daniel Charisi's grandson.[42]

The testaments of those two dying characters, Mordecai and Deronda's mother, are the highlights of the book, the set pieces that make it so powerful a novel and so formidable an intellectual discourse (and, in the confessions of Deronda's mother, so intriguing about Eliot herself). Everything that follows is almost anti-climactic. Some of the critics who are impatient with the Jewish part would have Deronda marry Gwendolen—"by far, the more suitable wife for Deronda."[43] Certainly Gwendolen would have had it that way. Deronda does all he can to comfort her after Grandcourt's death and to suggest a new way of life, a life lived for others which will give meaning to her own life. But he himself, he tells her, is destined for another love—and another kind of life.

> "I am going to the East to become better acquainted with the condition of my race in various countries there. . . . The idea that I am possessed with is that of restoring a political existence to my people, making them a nation again, giving them a national centre, such as the English have, though they too are scattered over the face of the globe. That is a task which presents itself to me as a duty: I am resolved to begin it, however feebly. I am resolved to devote my life to it. At the least, I may awaken a movement in other minds, such as has been awakened in my own."[44]

Deronda marries Mirah and prepares for their voyage East. The novel concludes at this point, with Ezra (as he is now called), satisfied that Deronda will fulfill his mission: "Where thou goest, Daniel, I shall go. Is it not begun? Have I not breathed my soul into you? We shall live together." Saying the *Shema*, he dies in the arms of Deronda and Mirah. The final words of the novel, however, are neither Ezra's, nor Deronda's, not even a Jewish sage's, but a quotation (not identified as such) from Milton's *Samson Agonistes*:

> Nothing is here for tears, nothing to wail
> Or knock the breast; no weakness, no contempt,
> Dispraise, or blame; nothing but well and fair,
> And what may quiet us in a death so noble.

POSTSCRIPT

"what's in a name?"

Mordecai does not explain why he chose to be known in England as Mordecai rather than Ezra, his familial name. For George Eliot's purpose, however, and in the context of the novel, the change from Mordecai to Ezra is significant.

There is a clear intimation in the novel itself that in naming her character Mordecai, Eliot had in mind the biblical Mordecai, the hero of the *Book of Esther*, who saved the Jews in Persia from the murderous Haman. When Deronda is at dinner with the Cohens and Mr. Cohen calls to Mordecai, their house guest, to come to the table, Deronda wonders whether invoking the name of that "ancient hero" is part of the religious ceremony of the Sabbath dinner, like the washing of hands.[45]

There is no similar allusion in the novel to the biblical Ezra, the hero of the *Book of Ezra*. But there are several references to him in Eliot's *Notebooks*, where Ezra appears as one of the chief *Sopherim* (scribes) in Jerusalem who helped rebuild the "Great Synagogue," restored the Torah and prayer book, enacted ordinances about intermarriage and Jewish identity, and began the tradition of oral law that culminated in the *Mishnah*.[46] Above all, Ezra is remembered as having led thousands of Jews out of Babylon and into Jerusalem. Were there, Eliot asked in her last essay, "some new Ezras, some modern Maccabees," to restore the Jewish people as a proper nation?[47]

The differences between the biblical Mordecai and the fictional one are obvious, and deliberately so. The biblical Mordecai was strong and triumphant, succeeding not only in rescuing the Jews in Persia but also in becoming a power in the land, rich and influential, "second to the king." The fictional Mordecai is frail and sickly, barely able to support himself, and agonizing over his failure to communicate his message of faith and redemption to the Jewish community. Yet he is firm in his conviction that he possesses the soul of his ancestors, and, in spite of his physical infirmities, he has the strength of mind and character to persist in his aims and to enlist Deronda in his cause. He is, in fact, as Deronda recognizes at their first meeting, even before he knows his name, "a prophet of the Exile."[48] That prophetic nature comes closer to fulfillment when, late in the book, Mordecai is restored to his own family under his proper familial name of Ezra—and closer still when Deronda himself, shortly afterwards, discovers his own identity as a Jew, making him worthy of the task Mordecai has laid upon him. Assured of his surrogate Deronda, Mordecai, on his deathbed, can rest in peace, confident that his alter ego, Ezra, will finally prevail.

Deronda himself experiences a similar transformation, in name as well as religion. He discovers not only that he is a Jew—and a Sephardi Jew at that, regarded as the most prestigious of Jews—but also that he is living under an assumed name. Charisi, not Deronda, is his real name; and his mother's professional name was Alcharisi. What neither his mother nor Kalonymus tells him is the source of that name. Kalonymus hints at it when he tells him that his grandfather, Daniel Charisi, "mingled all sorts of learning, and in that he was like our Arabic writers in the golden time."[49] But he does not mention the fact that one of those Arabic writers was Judah Alcharisi (today generally spelt Al-Harizi), who translated Maimonides's *Guide to the Perplexed* into Hebrew. Excerpts from the *Guide* are in Eliot's *Notebooks;* her own copy was a French translation. Deronda has good reason to be proud of his heritage, and not only because it was Sephardi.

The name of Deronda's informant, Joseph Kalonymos, is also rooted in history. Kalonymos describes himself as a great friend of Daniel Charisi, bound together, from their youth, by a vow of friendship. Charisi, he insists, was more learned than he, more thoughtful about his religion and the future of his people, but they were both faithful Jews proud of their heritage. About Charisi, Kalonymos says only (but this is a great compliment) that he was like the old Arabic sages. About his own forefathers he is more explicit. "The days are changed for us in Mainz since . . . Karl the Great [Charlemagne] fetched my ancestors from Italy to bring some tincture of knowledge to our rough German brethren."[50] In her *Notebooks*, in almost the same words, Eliot quoted (in German) and paraphrased (in English) the historian Graetz on the Kalonymos family: "Charles the Great patronizes the Jews and calls the Kalonymos from Lucca to Mainz, to spread knowledge among them."[51] When she received proofs of her book, she complained to her publisher: "The printers have sadly spoiled the beautiful Greek name Kalonymos, which was the name of a celebrated family of scholarly Jews

transplanted from Italy into Germany in medieval times." [52]
Her writing, she suggested, may have been faulty. But her
knowledge of Jewish history was not.

A final intriguing note: In the Hebrew Bible, between the
Book of Esther and the *Book of Ezra* appears the *Book of
Daniel*—the biblical Daniel, in the diaspora, prophecying the
return to Jerusalem. It is tempting to think that Eliot had that
Daniel in mind when she named her hero Daniel Deronda
(née Daniel Charisi), and assigned him the task of mediating
(as in a sense did the biblical Daniel) between Mordecai and
Ezra.

IV.

"HEP! HEP! HEP!"

a sequel to Daniel Deronda

Any temptation one might have had to relegate *Daniel Deronda* to the realm of fantasy (as one might Disraeli's novels) would be dissipated by a remarkable essay Eliot wrote two years after its publication. *Daniel Deronda* was her last novel, *Impressions of Theophrastus Such* her last book, and "The Modern Hep! Hep! Hep!" the last essay in that book. She started writing the book in June 1878 and completed it in November, reading it aloud to Lewes while he was sick. The last letter he wrote, enclosed with the manuscript to her publisher (he was her agent to the end), explained that this was "*not* a story."[1] Two days before he died, he had the satisfaction of seeing sample pages of the proofs and approved them. In February, three months after his death, Eliot told her publisher that she wanted to delay publication for a long time, finding it intolerable to have a book of hers appear so soon after his death. She later had second thoughts and agreed to its publication in May. "There are some things in it which I want to get said."[2] A year and a half later, on December 22, 1980, she died.

The book was well described by its working title, "Characters and Characteristics." Most of the essays were casual pieces on assorted characters—a country parson, a Liberal, a financier . . .—and reflections on recent cultural and social tendencies. The published title was recondite: *Impressions of Theophrastus Such*. Theophrastus was mentioned in passing in the second essay but not identified; Eliot may have thought it insulting to her readers to explain that he was Aristotle's successor in the Peripatetic School and the author of *Characters*, a book of sketches of social and moral types. Nor was the title of the last and longest essay, "The Modern Hep! Hep! Hep!" explained. That expression, "Hep! Hep! Hep!" appeared in *Daniel Deronda* in the course of a description of Deronda's wanderings in the Jewish neighborhoods of London. Eliot imagined him transported back to the Rhineland at the end of the eleventh century, when "the Hep! Hep! Hep! of the Crusaders came like the bay of bloodhounds" and the missionaries with "sword and firebrand" fell upon the Jews.[3] More recently (Eliot did not mention this but she may have had it in mind), "Hep! Hep!" had been the rallying cry of anti-Semitic rioters in Germany in 1819.[*]

---

* That event was well remembered in Germany, if not in England. Moses Hess referred to it in *Rome and Jerusalem*, published in 1862: "The Germans, after the Wars of Liberation, not only discriminated against the Jews, their erstwhile comrades in arms against the French, but even persecuted them with the frequent cries of Hep, Hep." The origins of the phrase are obscure. It is generally assumed that "Hep" was an acronym for "Hierosolyma est perdita" ("Jerusalem is lost"), the battle cry of the crusaders. It was also the cry of goat-herders in southern Germany. Cynthia Ozick adopted Eliot's title, "The Modern Hep! Hep! Hep!" as the title of her afterword to *Those Who Forget the Past: The Question of Anti-Semitism*, ed. Ron Rosenbaum (New York, 2004).

It has often been noted that *Daniel Deronda* is the only one of Eliot's novel to be set in the present. The essay "The Modern Hep! Hep! Hep!" has an even greater contemporary focus, taking the Jewish theme outside the realm of fiction and bringing it into the real world. It also put Judaism (and Zionism, to use that anachronistic word) in the larger context of nationality, the national identity that Eliot attributed to all great peoples—England most notably, but also Greece and Italy, which, in reasserting their nationality, were seeking to return to the forefront of history. For all peoples, Eliot said, the idea of nationality was elevating. "The eminence, the nobleness of a people depends on its capability of being stirred by memories, and of striving for what we call spiritual ends—ends which consist not in immediate material possession, but in the satisfaction of a great feeling that animates the collective body as with one soul." It was not only the collective soul that was thus ennobled by the "national consciousness." It was also the soul of each citizen, who was related to something larger than himself, "something great, admirable, pregnant with high possibilities, worthy of sacrifice, a continual inspiration to self-repression and discipline by the presentation of aims larger and more attractive to our generous part than the securing of personal ease or prosperity." As if anticipating the experiences of later generations, Eliot struck an even more modern note. "A common humanity is not yet enough to feed the rich blood of various activity which makes a complete man. The time is not come for cosmopolitanism to be highly virtuous, any more than for communism to suffice for social energy."[4]

Having established nationality as a universal principle, Eliot went on to apply it to the Jews, "a people whose ideas have determined the religion of half the world, and that the more cultivated half." The Hebrew canon, whether interpreted as revelation or as ancient literature, revealed a people whose national traditions were of the highest social and religious order, and whose sense of separateness was "unique in its intensity."* Unique in its intensity, Eliot pointed out, but not—before the dispersion, at least—in its essential qualities, for England had acquired its island much as the Israelites had acquired Canaan, and the Puritans, steeped in the Hebrew Scriptures, displayed the affinities of the English and Jewish races. After the dispersion, Jewish history became "more exceptional." Hunted and hounded, tortured and exiled, a people of weaker nature might have given way to pressure and merged with the population around them. Instead, tenaciously holding on to their inheritance of blood and faith, remembering their national glories and adhering to their spiritual obligations, the "kernel of their number" cherished all the more the differences that marked them off from their oppressors. "The separateness which was made their badge of ignominy would be their inward pride, their source of fortifying defiance."[5]

That separateness, unfortunately, also had the effect of confirming the Jews in their vices. Eliot conceded those vices while putting them in their social context. If Jews showed a talent for accumulating what Christians desired, Christians turned that to their own advantage by "mulcting or robbery,"

---

* The word "separateness," used repeatedly in her essay, appeared in *Daniel Deronda* as well, in the voice of Mordecai and again of Deronda's mother.

depriving them of their gains and preventing them from more acceptable pursuits such as agriculture or handicrafts. Or if Jews spat on the cross or held the name of Christ to be anathema, they were taught to do so by men who made Christianity "a curse to them" and who exacted vengeance upon them to satisfy their own "savageness, greed, and envy." Or if Jews exhibited signs of superiority and pride, these were the sources of their defiance and endurance. "An oppressive government and a persecuting religion, while breeding vices in those who hold power, are well known to breed answering vices in those who are powerless and suffering." Those "answering vices" were a condition of Jewish survival.[6]

It is certainly worth considering whether an expatriated, denationalised race, used for ages to live among antipathetic populations, must not inevitably lack some conditions of nobleness. If they drop that separateness which is made their reproach, they may be in danger of lapsing into a cosmopolitan indifference equivalent to cynicism. . . . Unquestionably the Jews, having been more than any other race exposed to the adverse moral influences of alienism, must, both in individuals and in groups, have suffered some corresponding moral degradation; but in fact they have escaped with less of abjectness and less of hard hostility towards the nations whose hand has been against them, than could have happened in the case of a people who had neither their adhesion to a separate religion founded on historic memories, nor their characteristic family affectionateness. Tortured, flogged, spit upon, the *corpus vile* on which rage or wantonness vented themselves with impunity, their name flung at them as an opprobrium by superstition, hatred, and contempt, they

have remained proud of their origin. Does any one call
this an evil pride?[7]

If Eliot was unsparing but also apologetic in her delinea-
tion of Jewish vices, she was effusive in her description of Jewish virtues. Thus pride, which in one sense might be regarded
as evil, was also a "humanizing, elevating habit of mind."
Other virtues—kindness and tenderness, the pity for orphans
and widows, the care for women and children, the love of
domestic life—had withstood centuries of persecution and
oppression because they were deeply ingrained in the Jewish
religion and race. Jews excelled in still other qualities that
made them the rivals of all European countries: healthiness
and strong physique, practical ability, and scientific and artistic aptitude. Their "natural rank" among peoples was such
that a Jew was the leader of the Liberal party in Germany,
of the Republican party in France, and of the Conservative
ministry in England. But this too was cause for jealousy and
the revival of old antipathies.[8]

People complained that Jews were "carrying off the best
prizes" and that their wealth could put "half the seats in Parliament at their disposal." Similar arguments, Eliot pointed
out, were made about other immigrant groups, and, for that
matter, about the Scots, who were said to be more numer-
ous and prosperous in the South than the English liked, or
the Irish who were too hungry and hard-working. Surely, she
protested, no one was proposing to repeal the laws emanci-
pating the Jews. It would be a calamity if a premature infusion
of immigrants of "alien blood" had the effect of obliterating
the country's distinctive national characteristics. But to turn
away the peaceful foreigner would be against the interests of
the English themselves. The best course of action was to strive

for "fuller national excellence" by producing "more excellent individual natives." The "fusion of races" was inevitable. All that should be done was to bring it about moderately and gradually, so as not to degrade or efface the moral character and traditions that were the source of the national genius.[9]

The fusion of races was a problem for Jews as well. Were they destined to a complete fusion with the peoples among whom they lived, losing their distinctive consciousness as Jews? Or was there in them the intensity of that sense of separateness, of a national consciousness, that united Jewish communities throughout the world? And were there, in the present or near future, the political conditions for the restoration of a Jewish state that would serve as "a centre of national feeling, a source of dignifying protection, a special channel for special energies which may contribute some added form of national genius"—and, Eliot added, would also serve as a "voice in the councils of the world?" Some Jews, the wealthiest Jews, might not wish to forsake their "European palaces" and go to live in Jerusalem, just as many prosperous Jews had remained in Babylon when Ezra marshaled his band of forty thousand and began a "new glorious epoch in the history of his race," and an epoch, too, "in the history of the world." The question was whether there were today enough worthy Jews, "some new Ezras, some modern Maccabees," who, by their heroic example, would triumph over the indifference or scorn of others and set about making their people "once more one among the nations."[10]

The idea of the "restoration of the Jews," Eliot recalled, had been endorsed by Evangelicals as the fulfillment of the sacred Biblical prophecy. Those Christians who disowned that prophecy were disowning their own origin. "The Jews were steadfast in their separateness, and through that separateness

Christianity was born." In support of this argument for separateness, Eliot invoked an unlikely authority, John Stuart
Mill. "A modern book on Liberty has maintained that from
the freedom of individual men to persist in idiosyncrasies the
world may be enriched. Why should we not apply this argument to the idiosyncrasy of a nation?" That "idiosyncrasy"
was the source and strength of the Jewish nation, the bond
that held together those who bore the "triple name of Hebrew,
Israelite, and Jew."[11]

> There is still a great function for the steadfastness of the
> Jew: not that he should shut out the utmost illumination
> which knowledge can throw on his national history, but
> that he should cherish the store of inheritance which that
> history has left him. Every Jew should be conscious that
> he is one of a multitude possessing common objects of
> piety in the immortal achievements and immortal sorrows
> of ancestors who have transmitted to them a physical and
> mental type strong enough, eminent enough in faculties,
> pregnant enough with peculiar promise, to constitute a
> new beneficent individuality among the nations, and, by
> confuting the traditions of scorn, nobly avenge the wrongs
> done to their Fathers.[12]

The boldness of this theme—Judaism as a race, a nation, and
potentially a state—has obscured other aspects of the essay
that reveal how far Eliot had come in her intellectual and
political odyssey. It implied, for one thing, a repudiation of
Strauss and Feuerbach, who had played so large a part in her

early life and work.[13] In a sense, they were the silent antagonists in the debate she was conducting both in the novel and in the essay. When Gideon and Lilly, at the Philosophers club, objected to Jewish "separateness," "exclusiveness," "arrogance," and "obstinate adherence to the superannuated," they were echoing, often in their very words, the charges made by Strauss and Feuerbach (although, being English, they did so with far less venom). Mordecai responded by turning their arguments against them, making virtues out of what they saw as vices. In the essay, Eliot adopted the same strategy, the conventional indictment of Judaism becoming a spirited defense of it—and this without ever mentioning the names of Strauss or Feuerbach. Where the latter had disowned all religion as mythical and illusory, with Judaism the most retrograde form of religion, Eliot praised Judaism not only as the vital source of Jewish nationality but also as the origin of Christianity, thus vindicating Christianity along with Judaism—and religion along with nationality. In affirming what they condemned, Eliot was coming to terms with her own past, recanting some of the beliefs that had once captivated her imagination and her mind.

So, too, Eliot put Spinoza behind her, more explicitly but also more equivocally. When a reviewer of *Daniel Deronda*, recalling the discussion club Lewes had belonged to, suggested that another member of that club, the watch-maker Cohn, was the model for Mordecai, Eliot sharply denied it. Cohn, she pointed out, was of the "Spinoza type," in marked contrast to Mordecai.[14] Mordecai himself, arguing in his club for "another great migration, another choosing of Israel to be a nationality," invoked the example of Spinoza. "Baruch Spinoza had not a faithful Jewish heart, though he had sucked the life of his intellect at the breasts of Jewish tradition." Yet even Spinoza "saw not why Israel should not again be a chosen nation."[15]

Those were damning words—Spinoza "had not a faithful Jewish heart"—somewhat redeemed, however, by the remark (couched in negatives) about Israel as a "chosen nation." Mordecai was clearly alluding to a passage in the third chapter of the *Tractatus Theologico-Politicus* (Eliot may have reached that chapter before abandoning her translation) in which Spinoza said that the mark of circumcision was in itself of such great importance as to preserve the Jewish people for ever. "Indeed, did not the principles of their religion make them effeminate, I should be quite convinced that some day when opportunity arises—so mutable are human affairs— they will establish their state once more, and that God will choose them afresh."[16]

For Eliot, Spinoza was not simply the renegade from Judaism, the rationalist philosopher who rejected the traditions and dogmas of Judaism, as of all religions. This Spinoza, Eliot (like Mordecai) clearly rejected. But she was aware of a more complicated Spinoza, who recognized Judaism as a people and could foresee and approve of the restoration of Israel as a nation—a secular, democratic nation, he insisted. It was this Spinoza whom David Ben-Gurion, seeking to lift the ban placed on Spinoza in the seventeenth century by the Amsterdam Jewish community, proclaimed the "greatest and most original thinker" of the Jewish people.[17]

Even in her early years, when Eliot was part of the radical circle first in Coventry and then in London, her radicalism was more philosophical and theological than political or social. Indeed, in disposition and temperament, she was, even then, something of a conservative.[18] While vigorously disputing Disraeli, for example, on the subject of Jews, she confessed that she was well disposed to him in other respects. In 1845, after reading *Sybil*, she ventured to tell Mrs. Bray, herself a good radical, that she was "not utterly disgusted with D'Israeli. The man hath good veins, as Bacon would say, but there is not enough blood in them."[19] Three years later, while sharply criticizing *Tancred*, she acknowledged Disraeli as "unquestionably an able man." "I always enjoy his tirades against liberal principles as opposed to *popular* principles—the name by which he distinguishes his own."[20]

By the mid-Sixties, Eliot had deviated so far from conventional liberalism, let alone radicalism, as to sound very much like a Tory—a "Tory Democrat," perhaps, of the Disraeli mode. The labor leader in her novel, *Felix Holt, the Radical,* was so little a radical that, as one commentator observed, the novel could as well have been called "Felix Holt, the Conservative."[21] Published in 1866, when the Second Reform Bill was being debated, the novel itself was set in 1831, when the First Reform Bill was even more hotly debated. Opposing the franchise, Felix Holt argued that the well-being of the workers depended not on this or that political reform but on their own moral character and on that of society at large. Eliot's publisher, John Blackwood, a good Tory, was delighted with the book. "I suspect I am a radical of the Felix Holt breed," he told her, "and so was my father before me."[22] The following year, after hearing Disraeli's speech on the Second Reform Bill, he suggested that Eliot write a speech on the same subject, ostensibly delivered by the hero of her novel. "Address to Working Men, by Felix Holt," published early in 1868, transmitted the message of the novel to those workers who had just received the franchise. Warning them that the vote was no cure for their ills, Felix Holt urged them to abandon the idea of class interest in favor of the common interest of society, to regard duties as paramount to interests, and to consider the overriding need for public order. "What I am striving to keep in our minds," Holt told them, "is the care, the precaution, with which we should go about making things better, so that the public order may not be destroyed, so that no fatal shock may be given to this society of ours, this living body in which our lives are bound up."[23] It was a message that might have been delivered by Disraeli himself.[*]

Eliot's admiration for Disraeli was accompanied by a deep distaste for his rival. During one ministerial crisis in 1873, while Gladstone was prime minister, she wished that there was "a solid, philosophical Conservative to take the reins, one who knows the true functions of stability in human affairs, and as the psalm says, 'would also practise what he knows.'"[25] She was pleased when the election the following year returned Disraeli to power. "I who am no believer in Salvation by Ballot, am rather tickled that the first experiment with it has turned against its adherents."[26] She approved of Disraeli's conduct of foreign affairs and praised him for his success at the Congress of Berlin in 1878 in resisting the expansion of Russian power. To the French translator of *Romola* she spoke of her satisfaction with the outcome of

---

[*] The Reform Bill of 1867, introduced and passed in Disraeli's administration, was more comprehensive than that originally proposed by the Liberals. This was not because Disraeli was a great believer in the franchise, but because he had great faith in the conservative instincts of the working class and in the Tory Party as the "national" party and "natural" leaders of the working class. Although the Conservatives lost the election of 1868, they won that of 1874 and afterwards more than held their own, with the help of a working-class electorate.[24]

that crisis. "You remember me as much less of a conservative than I have now become. I care as much or more for the interests of the people, but I believe less in the help they will get from democrats."[27] Later, she rebuked her old friend Edith Simcox for calling Disraeli unprincipled and expressed her disgust with the "venom" of the speeches by Gladstone and other Liberals. She even went so far as to call Disraeli's novels "wonderfully clever."[28]

Eliot's conservatism—a cultural and social as well as a political conservativism—displayed itself in another episode that sharply distinguished her from her liberal friends. At the very time that Felix Holt was arguing against the Reform Bill of 1867 enfranchising the working class, Eliot was refusing to support John Stuart Mill's amendment to the same bill which would have enfranchised women.[*] Her refusal surprised the feminists who assumed that her interest in higher education for women (she was a sponsor of Girton College in Cambridge), as well as her unconventional relationship with Lewes, would have made her a natural ally in their cause. Instead, as she explained to John Morley, who had solicited her endorsement of the bill, she believed that while "zoological evolution" had given women "the worse share in existence," "moral evolution" had endowed them with "'an art which does amend nature.'"[†] That "art" was love. "It is the function of love in the largest sense to mitigate the harshness of all fatalities. And in the thorough recognition of that worse

---

[*] Eliot was not the only woman writer to oppose the enfranchisement of women. A petition supporting Mill's amendment was signed by 1500 women, but not by Charlotte Bronte, Mrs. Gaskell, Elizabeth Barrett Browning, Christina Rossetti, Charlotte Yonge, and Margaret Oliphant. Florence Nightingale also refused to sign.[29]

[†] This is a quotation from Shakespeare's *The Winter's Tale*.

share, I think there is a basis for a sublimer resignation in woman and a more regenerating tenderness in man."[30]

In *Theophrastus Such,* that conservatism emerged most explicitly. The father of the narrator in the essay "Looking Backward" was a Tory of the old school, who regarded "innovators and dissenters" as persons of "ill-founded self-confidence." He had nothing but contempt for those of his contemporaries, like Wordsworth, who greeted the French Revolution with enthusiasm and believed in the "speedy regeneration of all things." He himself had the highest regard for government, indeed, for a strong government, a government that would promote the welfare of the nation by maintaining order. "I was accustomed," his son remembered, "to hear him utter the word 'Government' in a tone that charged it with awe, and made it part of my effective religion." The son, more urbane and sophisticated than the father, was conscious of his own "conservative prepossessions." "Our national life," he reflected, "is like that scenery which I early learned to love, not subject to great convulsions but easily showing more or less delicate (sometimes melancholy) effects from minor changes. Hence our midland plains have never lost their familiar expression and conservative spirit for me." Even as he learned to admire foreign countries and London itself, so different from the pastoral world of his youth, the son never lost sight of the familiar plains and hills of his youth. "I cherish my childish loves, the memory of that warm little nest where my affections were fledged."[31]

One is reminded of *Daniel Deronda,* of the time when Gwendolen returned home, after the gambling episode, only to find that she had no real home, no "spot of a native land" where she might feel "the love of tender kinship for the face of the earth," no place where "early memories may be inwrought with affection."[32] That quest for identity, a religious and national identity, is the unifying theme of the book. Indeed, the whole of *Daniel Deronda* was imbued with the same spirit. Judaism, as Deronda understood it, was a living, "throbbing" faith precisely because it had its roots in ancient traditions and laws, in enduring habits and sentiments; it was these that made the Jews a "nation" deserving of a "polity." Deronda did not feel the need to redefine or update Judaism to accommodate the idea of a state. He did not invoke a new version of Judaism—a "reformed" or "liberal" or "reconstructed" Judaism. His was a traditional Judaism rooted in the past, an inheritance (like the inheritance of his grandfather's chest) that bound together all Jews, at all times and places, in a single nation.

As Deronda cherished his Jewish nationality, so he also cherished the English nationality that was his (and his mother's) by birth, as well as by a long and loving association. Both as a Jew and as an Englishman, he was, Eliot made clear, "intensely conservative." "He was fervidly democratic in his feeling for the multitude, and yet, through his affections and imagination, intensely conservative; voracious of speculations on government and religion, yet loath to part with long-sanctioned forms which, for him, were quick with memories and sentiments that no argument could lay dead."[33] Even Sir Hugo, a good party Liberal, was a conservative by instinct and temperament. "For Sir Hugo was a man who liked to show himself and be affable, a Liberal of good lineage, who confided entirely in Reform as not likely to make any serious difference in English habits of feeling, one of which undoubtedly is the liking to behold society well fenced and adorned with hereditary rank."[34] (He might have been echoing Disraeli, who supported the Reform Act in much the same spirit.)

Theophrastus Such restated, more prosaically and less dramatically, the central theme of *Daniel Deronda*. It was Eliot's final testament, her bequest to the Jews (as Mordecai's was to Deronda)—and to the world as well.

V.

THE RECEPTION *of*
DANIEL DERONDA

From the beginning, the "Jewish element" in *Daniel Deronda* was seen as a problem. In February 1876, when the first serial part was published, Eliot, anticipating criticism, thought that most novel readers would be more interested in Sidonia (Disraeli's character) than in Mordecai. "But then," she told her publisher, John Blackwood, "I was not born to paint Sidonia"; she was striving for a "more complex character and a higher strain of ideas."[1]* Perhaps to allay her fears, after the appearance of the second part, Blackwood wrote Lewes praising "the marvellous Mordecai and oh that Cohen family!"[3] The following month, although satisfied with the sales (which were somewhat better than *Middlemarch* at a corresponding point), Eliot still had doubts about the public response to the story. "The Jewish element," she confided in her journal, was "likely to satisfy nobody."[4] Lewes tried to reassure Blackwood, as well as Eliot, that the Jewish element

---

* Disraeli's famous quip "When I want to read a novel, I write one" was said in response to the question whether he had read *Daniel Deronda*.[2]

was more popular than they had expected, but they knew better.[5] By the time the serial publication was completed, Blackwood confessed to Eliot that he always knew that the "strong Jew element" would be unpopular, but was pleased that it was helping overcome the public distaste for the Jewish characters and that it was being discussed as if it were "a great historical event."[6]

When one of Eliot's American admirers, Harriet Beecher Stowe (the author of *Uncle Tom's Cabin*), congratulated her on *Daniel Deronda*, adding that she preferred the English half to the Jewish half, Eliot responded at length and with passion.[*]

> As to the Jewish element in 'Deronda,' I expected from
> first to last in writing it, that it would create much stron-
> ger resistance, and even repulsion, than it has actually met
> with. But precisely because I felt that the usual attitude
> of Christians towards Jews is—I hardly know whether
> to say more impious or more stupid when viewed in the
> light of their professed principles, I therefore felt urged
> to treat Jews with such sympathy and understanding as
> my nature and knowledge could attain to. Moreover,
> not only towards the Jews, but towards all Oriental
> peoples with whom we English come in contact, a spirit
> of arrogance and contemptuous dictatorialness is observ-
> able which has become a national disgrace to us. There
> is nothing I should care more to do, if it were possible,
> than to rouse the imagination of men and women to a

---

[*] Harriet Stowe's belittling of the Jewish half may have surprised Eliot, because Calvin Stowe, her husband, was a respected Hebrew scholar, the author of *The Origin and History of the Books of the Bible*. Mrs. Stowe referred to him as her "Rabbi."

vision of human claims in those races of their fellow-men who most differ from them in customs and beliefs. But towards the Hebrews we western people, who have been reared in Christianity, have a peculiar debt, and whether we acknowledge it or not, a peculiar thoroughness of fellowship in religion and moral sentiment. Can anything be more disgusting than to hear people called 'educated' making small jokes about eating ham, and showing themselves empty of any real knowledge as to the relations of their own social and religious life to the history of the people they think themselves witty in insulting? They hardly know that Christ was a Jew. . . . The best that can be said of it is that it is a sign of the intellectual narrowness—in plain English, the stupidity—which is still the average mark of our culture.[7]

Lewes shielded Eliot from most of the reviews, showing her only excerpts that might please or entertain her. But she was fully aware that the Jewish part was being received with repugnance or, at best, indifference. She took some comfort in its reception among Jews, who were delighted with the portrayal of Jews and, more important to her, confirmed its accuracy. The Deputy Chief Rabbi of Britain (later the Chief Rabbi) expressed his appreciation of "the fidelity with which some of the best traits of the Jewish character" were depicted.[8*] Another leader of the Jewish community, thanking her for presenting Jews in so agreeable and scholarly a manner, enclosed his Hebrew translation of the Philosophers club

---

* The "best traits" of the Jewish character were perhaps not what Freud had in mind when he read the novel a few years later. He was amazed, he told his wife, by its revelation of Jewish intimate ways that "we speak of only among ourselves."[9]

scene, which was published in a Jewish paper in Lemberg, together with a pamphlet reporting on recent discussions of the financing and establishing of a Jewish colony in Palestine. Lewes reported on other letters from "learned Jews and impassioned Jewesses," in Germany, Poland, and France, as well as England and America, who assured her that she had "really touched and set vibrating a deep chord."[10]

Some of the reviews were both favorable and serious enough for her to read in their entirety. A long essay in a German scholarly journal by David Kaufmann, a professor at the Jewish Theological Seminary in Budapest, prompted a warm letter of thanks. She told him that in spite of the "prejudice and ignorant obtuseness" she had met with, she had not repented her choice of subject or her effort to bring an "ennobling" Judaism to the consciousness of Christians and Jews.[11] (Kaufmann's essay, "George Eliot and Judaism," was translated into English and published by Blackwood the following year.) Lewes might also have shown her the review in the *Jewish Chronicle* praising her for presenting a new image of the Jew—not the conventional literary Jew, "spat upon, trampled under foot, trembling for his life, honour and property," but a Jew "dwelling in safety, freed from the ghetto, come into contact with modern civilization and culture." It was just such a Jew who could aspire to the future envisioned by Mordecai.[12]

Successive reviews in one journal, both favorable, were so different that they might have been discussing different books. The first praised Eliot for writing a great "Romance" (capitalized), not about ordinary people in the actual world, but about "the truth that lies in the well of dreams."[13] A review in the next issue, by James Picciotto (a Jewish historian), praised her even more effusively for writing a novel about Jews which went beyond the "romance-writer's skill." Unlike most other novels (by Dickens, Trollope, and Disraeli as well) with their caricatures of Jews, hers was about the customs and speech of real Jews. The portrait of the Cohen family was a "photographic likeness" probably taken from life; Ezra Cohen, the pawnbroker, was an embodiment of the qualities, "good and indifferent," of the Jewish tradesman"; and Mordecai, "a prophet, a seer," was not at all the "impossible character" some critics had made him out to be. In spite of their mercantile pursuits, Picciotto reminded his readers, Jews had always produced thinkers and philosophers. As if to confirm the veracity of the novel, he cited an article by G. H. Lewes (not identified as Eliot's husband) describing a club to which he had belonged which was very much like Mordecai's Philosophers club.[14]*

The reception of *Daniel Deronda* by Jews was in stark contrast to most of the reviews, which, Eliot complained, "cut the book into scraps and talk of nothing in it but Gwendolen."[15] A common criticism was that the characters were analyzed and moralized rather than painted and observed. The distinguished jurist A. V. Dicey complained that while all of Eliot's novels had a moral purpose, here it was predominant.

---

* Picciotto did find "some slight errors" in the novel about the prayer for the dead, which did not, he insisted, detract from the "marvellous accuracy" of the scenes. (These errors, and others pointed out by Kaufmann, were corrected in the second edition in 1878.) He also thought it strange (as some later readers have) that Deronda himself should never have "suspected his origin, which ought to have left visible traces." But perhaps Deronda's mother and acquiescent husband had prevailed against the wishes of her father and did not have the child circumcised.

"Instead of the action of a drama telling its own tale, you have the reflective comment of a chorus of moralists."[16] For Dicey, this insistent moralizing impaired all the characters, Gwendolen as much as Deronda. For most reviewers, it applied only to the Jewish characters. Gwendolen and Grandcourt were seen as fully realized human beings, while Deronda and Mordecai were stock figures, the artificial contrivances of the author.

There was an almost schizophrenic tone in many of the reviews: the believable characters (the English) versus the unbelievable (the Jewish), the brilliant Eliot versus the failed Eliot. Even the style was implicated in this great divide, the Jewish sections said to be labored and sententious, the English lucid and realistic. The review by the respected critic George Saintsbury fell almost exactly into this pattern, contrasting the "wonderful creations" of Gwendolen and Grandcourt to the "priggish" Deronda (who was not only dislikeable but also impossible), the "exquisite" picture of a passing wagon to the Jewish scenes devoid of any "fellow feeling," anything "broadly human." Saintsbury concluded with the reminder of the immutable law of fiction, that no perfect novel could be written merely to illustrate a theory.[17]

For some reviewers, the Jewish theme was so dominant as to vitiate the whole of the book. With only the obligatory reference to Eliot's "distinctive excellences," the *Saturday Review* critic found the book so foreign, so outside the realm of ordinary concerns and motives, as to preclude any sympathy with the characters or theme. "What can be the design of this ostentatious separation from the universal instinct of Christendom, this subsidence into Jewish hopes and aims?" A reader could only respond with "bewilderment and affront" to this young man of English training, education, and assumed birth who ends up married in a Jewish synagogue because his father was a Jew. The reviewer himself was bewildered and affronted by the simultaneous appearance of the last part of *Daniel Deronda* and the first of a series of papers "On the Liturgy of the Jews, by a Jew"—this in a popular journal where the subject of Judaism was "most curiously incongruous." (The unnamed journal was the *Pall Mall Gazette*.)[18]

A more sympathetic review made the novel seem less foreign by humanizing and universalizing Judaism, insisting that the religion was not miraculous or supernatural, implied no personal providence, and derived its faith entirely from the spirit of man. "Human life itself is shown to be sacred, a temple with its shrines for devout humility and aspiration." It was of this benign Judaism that Mordecai was the prophet and Deronda the anointed priest. "The Judaic element comes second in the book," the reviewer explained, "the human element first."[19] In the same spirit, another reviewer (unsigned, but identified as Richard Hutton) praised the religion depicted in the book as "a purified Judaism, in other words, a devout Theism, purged of Jewish narrowness, while retaining the intense patriotism which pervades Judaism." Hutton, himself a theologian, demurred only with Mordecai's assumption that there was nothing in the teaching of Christ that raised Christianity above Judaism. Mordecai himself was something of a puzzle, reminding Hutton of Disraeli and the "great Asiatic mystery," except that Mordecai's moral nature was "much more noble and definite than anything of which Mr. Disraeli ever caught a glimpse."[20]

The most memorable review (memorable for itself as well as its author) was by a friend of Eliot and Lewes. Henry James had earlier reviewed almost all of Eliot's novels, admiringly but not uncritically—and, of course, anonymously. (Had she known he had written them, he might not have been so welcome a visitor at their house.)* James's review of the first installment of *Daniel Deronda* was favorable. The finished novel was another matter. Perhaps inspired by the discussion at the Philosophers club, he cast his review in the form of a conversation with three protagonists: Pulcheria, who was unremittingly critical; Theodora, entirely admiring; and Constantius (James's alter ego), mediating between them. Pulcheria, frankly anti-Semitic (Jews were "dirty" and had "big Jewish noses"), found the book "protracted, pretentious, pedantic." People were described and analyzed to death, but they were not seen or heard or touched. Deronda was "a dreadful prig" and Gwendolen was not much better, "a second-rate English girl who got into a flutter about a lord." Theodora was as enthusiastic as Pulcheria was derisive. She confessed herself hopelessly in love with Deronda, the "most irresistible man" in fiction, an ideal character yet "triumphantly married to reality."

The final judgment rested with Constantius. He agreed with Pulcheria that most of the characters were based on

---

* James's description of Eliot, in a letter to his father after their first meeting, would surely have made him *persona non grata*. "To begin with she is magnificently ugly—deliciously hideous. She has a low forehead, a dull grey eye, a vast pendulous nose, a huge mouth, full of uneven teeth, and a chin and jaw-bone. . . . Now in this vast ugliness resides a most powerful beauty which, in a very few minutes steals forth and charms the mind, so that you end, as I ended, in falling in love with her."[21]

invention rather than observation, with the notable excep-
tions of Gwendolen and Grandcourt who were altogether
admirable, and Gwendolen in particular a masterpiece.
Deronda, Mordecai, and Mirah, on the other hand, were
only shadows, their stories entirely improvised. The subject
was a noble one, Constantius conceded, but Eliot, with her
admirable intellect, chose to deal with it as a philosopher and
moralist rather than as an observer and feeler. "She has given
a chill to her genius. She has come near spoiling an artist.
. . . All the Jewish part is at bottom cold." Deronda's mother
belonged to the "cold half of the book"; if James enjoyed her
story it was because his "fancy often warms cold things." But
beside Gwendolen's story, the mother's was "like the empty
half of the lunar disk beside the full one."[22]

That there was nothing anti-Semitic in James's critique
of the Jewish part was evident from the character of Pulcheria, an avowed and disagreeable anti-Semite who stood in
dramatic contrast to the decent and sensible Constantius. It
is also interesting that Constantius (and James, like many
other critics) entirely approved of another Jew in the novel,
the musician Klesmer, admitting him into the "good part" of
the novel—just as he was admitted, in the novel itself, into
the good part of society. A much admired musician who performed at soirées in the houses of the local gentry, Klesmer
was not only Jewish but foreign as well (German and Slavic
as well as Semitic)—the "Wandering Jew," as he ironically
referred to himself. Yet he did not think it amiss to court
a proper Christian lady (an heiress, to boot) who happily
returned his favors, and whose parents condoned their marriage after their initial objections. Critics had no problem
with this *mésalliance*, as they did with Deronda's marriage

to Mirah. They did not go so far as Theodora and Constantius, who compared Klesmer with Shakespeare. But they did regard him, like Gwendolen and Grandcourt, as a fully developed and credible character—credible, perhaps, because, as his fiancée explained, he was a Jew with "cosmopolitan ideas" who looked forward to a "fusion of races."[23] What the critics did not find credible was Mordecai's "separatist" creed of Judaism, and, still less credible, Deronda's willing adoption of that creed.

Eliot's death in 1880 and the publication five years later of Cross's biography (a compilation of her letters) were the occasion for reappraisals of her work and reputation. Even those obituary writers who were most respectful, even eulogistic, tended to bypass *Daniel Deronda*, as if unwilling to speak ill of the dead. James himself, in a long review of Cross's book, commented extensively and favorably on Eliot's other novels while dismissing *Daniel Deronda* briefly, with his familiar criticism of Deronda and Mirah (misspelt as Myra) and praise of Gwendolen and Grandcourt. Lord Acton, in a rhapsodic letter to Mary Gladstone, said that he received the news of Eliot's death as if "the sun had gone out." Declaring his enormous debt to her, he included her with such other luminaries as Shakespeare, Sophocles, and Dante—without mentioning *Daniel Deronda*.[24] Later, in a long review of Cross's biography, he lauded Eliot as "a consummate expert in the pathology of conscience"; the only references to *Daniel Deronda* were an epigraph to one of the chapters and speculation about the models for some of the characters.[25]

Leslie Stephen, a friend of Eliot's, opened his obituary essay by declaring that in her lifetime she was "the greatest living writer of English fiction," and that in death she was "the greatest woman who ever won literary fame." *Daniel Deronda* occupied a single sentence in that long essay, with Mordecai and Deronda described as "intolerable bores," and the Gwendolen-Grandcourt story as "a singularly powerful study of the somewhat repulsive kind."[26] In his biography of Eliot twenty-one years later, he found the Gwendolen story powerful although perhaps overly psychological (a fault the reader could easily remedy, Stephen said, by skipping a paragraph or two), and Deronda himself so "ethereal" that one was shocked to find him mentioned in connection with food. Eliot excelled, he said, in her portraits of women and in perceiving the feminine aspects of her male characters, but in Deronda she created not merely a feminine hero but a "schoolgirl's hero," an "amiable monomaniac" possessed with an untenable idea. Deronda, Stephen suggested, would have embodied Eliot's sentiments more perfectly if, instead of devoting himself to Jews, he had been a prophet in "the church of humanity"—a Positivist, in short, rather than a Jew.[27*]

Seventeen years later, Stephen's daughter, Virginia Woolf, overcoming her Bloomsbury disdain for all things Victorian, wrote an essay in the *Times Literary Supplement* celebrating Eliot on the centenary of her birth. It was then that Woolf

---

* The Positivist friend of Eliot, Frederic Harrison, could only account for her taking on so uncongenial a subject on the theory that Lewes was an "unconscious, unrecognized Gentile Jew in spirit." Lewes himself commented on the rumors that he was Jewish, and Eliot was often described as looking Jewish.[28]

made the memorable pronouncement about *Middlemarch*: "one of the few English novels written for grown-up people." Praising Eliot's portraits of her female characters, Woolf took them as testimony to her greatness, not only as a novelist but also as a woman who managed to surmount the considerable obstacles of "sex and health and convention." The eulogy concluded by bestowing upon Eliot a wreath of laurel and rose, the symbols of energy and passion.[29] Yet in this moving memorial, there was no mention of Eliot's last novel, *Daniel Deronda*.

Virginia Woolf's was a rare and unexpected tribute at that time. Eliot's reputation had been in decline since before the turn of the century. In 1895, George Saintsbury, who had earlier written an equivocal review of *Daniel Deronda*, reported that even the "coterie admiration" of Eliot had broken down, and although her novels might still be read, she was no longer held in critical esteem.[30] G. K. Chesterton, assessing Victorian literature on the eve of the war, compared the maturity of *Silas Marner* with the "analyzed dust-heaps" of *Daniel Deronda*.[31] After the war, Edmund Gosse could find nothing to praise even in *Middlemarch*, which he dismissed as mechanical and devoid of any reality. *Daniel Deronda* was worse still, its pedantry and pomposity alienating even her friends and admirers; he himself, Gosse announced, could find not a word to say in favor of it.[32] David Cecil, in 1935, judged Eliot only in negatives. Though a thinker, she was "not a particularly original thinker" and her loss of reputation was "not wholly undeserved." He graciously concluded that she was nevertheless a great writer, a "not unworthy heir" of Thackeray and Dickens and a "not unworthy forerunner" of Hardy and James.[33]

In America one might look to the two eminent twentieth-century critics for commentaries on *Daniel Deronda*. But one would do so in vain, for neither Edmund Wilson nor Lionel Trilling, both prolific essayists and reviewers, wrote about that novel or, indeed, about any of Eliot's novels. This is particularly odd in the case of Trilling, who was immersed in Victorian literature, who was as notable a moral critic as Eliot was a moral novelist, and who as a Jew might have been especially intrigued by *Daniel Deronda*. It is all the more odd because he was thoroughly familiar with her life and work. His first published book on Matthew Arnold quoted *Daniel Deronda* on the subject of race and *Felix Holt* on the idea of class, referred to Eliot's translation of Feuerbach, and was pleased to note her growing appreciation of Arnold's poetry. A footnote in a later essay on Keats cited a letter by her from Germany referring to Goethe's bad spelling. Trilling was also fond of quoting her remark about God, Immortality, and Duty, the first "inconceivable," the second "unbelievable," and the third "peremptory and absolute." Yet he never wrote the essay on *Daniel Deronda* or on Eliot that would have been so congenial to his own "moral imagination." What he did write, but did not publish, was an essay in which *Daniel Deronda* appeared toward the end, in four brief but intriguing pages.

In 1930, at the age of twenty-five, Trilling wrote an article for a Jewish magazine, the *Menorah Journal*, which was accepted and set in type but not published. Discovered many years later, it appeared posthumously in *Commentary* in 1978 under the title "The Changing Myth of the Jew," and was reprinted two years later in the final volume of his collected works. In that essay, Trilling traced the myth of the Jew from Chaucer, through the late-medieval miracle plays, Elizabethan drama, the romantic novels of the eighteenth century, and an assortment of novels in the nineteenth (by Scott, Dickens, Disraeli, Thackeray, and others). The essay concluded with a discussion of *Daniel Deronda*, "the last though certainly not the best novel of a novelist who in some ways stands very close to our own time."

For Trilling, *Daniel Deronda* enshrined the Jew in what became, to Jews at any rate, the most satisfactory "Jewish counter-myth," a repudiation of the earlier myths: the Jew as Judas, the hater of Christianity and lover of money; or the scheming, Machiavellian Jew of Marlowe and Shakespeare; or the devilish, demonic Wandering Jew of the Romantics; or the glamorous heroes of Disraeli's "race" of Jews. Eliot's characters—the Cohens, Mordecai, and Mirah—were meant to portray a quite different genre of Jews. But they too, Trilling observed, were mythical, embodying abstract traits rather than true individuals, and mythical, too, because they were intended to represent "the Jewish people," although English Jews were more diverse and less unanimously noble than Eliot pictured them. Yet they did have, Trilling conceded, a certain credibility. One could say of them, "Jews are like that," for some Jews, surely, had some of those traits to some degree. Moreover, Eliot visualized her Jews not only in relation to Gentiles and the Gentile world, as other novelists had, but as human beings living their own lives and coping with their own problems, especially the problem of assimilation. This was what Jewish readers responded to: "a genuine, inner, intimate quality" that, as much as the flattery, was acceptable to them and a model for later Jewish writers. The book was also noteworthy in advancing the idea of Zionism at a time when it was scarcely imagined. Eliot, in short, originated the counter-myth adopted by Jews themselves, which allowed them to present themselves "best foot foremost, to the world." It remained for a serious reader, Trilling concluded, to disentangle the mythical from the actual, a difficult task because in the mythical there is usually something of the truth.[34]

Trilling's essay is tantalizing, first because it reveals a greater familiarity than one might expect with the literary representation of Jews over the ages (the myths and counter-myths, as he saw them), and second, because the section on *Daniel Deronda* is so brief and, finally, unsatisfactory. Trilling had a great respect for the reality in fiction, the "actuality of the symbols" in Dickens's novels, for example—the fog in *Bleak House*, or the dust-heap and stench of the river in *Our Mutual Friend*.[35] But he also realized that the symbols themselves carried the weight of truth, the moral truth that went beyond the reality. It is surprising that Trilling chose not to publish this early essay, and more surprising that he never wrote an essay on *Daniel Deronda* itself, distinguishing the myth from the actuality and discovering (as he did in Dickens), the truth in the myth (or symbol) itself. Still more surprising is the fact that he never devoted an essay to Eliot, whom he must have admired not only as a moralist but also as an intellectual, two qualities that were conspicuously his own and that he valued in other writers. For his sake as much as for hers, one regrets this lacuna in his opus.

If Trilling was America's preeminent moral critic, F. R. Leavis was England's.* It was Leavis who revived interest in Eliot and restored her reputation, praising her as England's greatest novelist, and *Daniel Deronda*, in spite of its flaws, as the greatest of her novels. This process of rehabilitation started in 1945 with Leavis's essays on Eliot in *Scrutiny,* the influential literary journal he edited, and was reinforced three years later with the republication of those essays in *The Great Tradition.* Eliot occupied pride of place in that book, and thus in the "great tradition" of the novel itself. It was in that volume, too, that Henry James's "Conversation" appeared as an appendix, reinvigorating the debate about Eliot by reintroducing James as one of the great protagonists in that debate and the "Conversation" as one of its set pieces.

Leavis agreed with James's criticisms of the Jewish part of *Daniel Deronda*, but found the "good half" so magnificently good as to more than compensate for the "astonishing badness of the bad half." He made it clear (as not all critics did) that he had no problem with the ideas represented by Deronda or by Eliot's attraction to those ideas.† Her "generous moral fervour," he said, spontaneously engaged her

---

* Trilling has been represented as the American counterpart of Leavis, a characterization that displeased him because he had no very high regard for Leavis, finding him too parochial a literary critic and too narrow-minded a moralist. In his review of Leavis's *The Great Tradition*, Trilling made only passing references to Eliot, who occupied so prominent a place in that volume.[36]

† An essay on Leavis makes much of the fact that his wife and frequent collaborator, "Queenie," was Jewish, who had been repudiated by her Orthodox family when she married outside the faith. In her memoir of her husband, Q. D. Leavis said that he had originally omitted *Daniel Deronda* from his essay on Eliot and included it only after she gave him her copy of the book (which her parents had given her as a youngster), and pointed out to him "all the good things in the 'Gwendolen Harleth' part."[37]

in sympathy with Jews, and her religious as well as intellectual bent were naturally congenial to Jewish culture and history. "A distinguished mind and a noble nature" were unquestionably present in the bad part of *Daniel Deronda*, "but it *is* bad;" and the nobility, generosity, and moral idealism were simply "self-indulgence." It was self-indulgence that made Eliot will Deronda into existence, conceiving him in accord with her specifications and endowing him with the exaltation and fervors that she herself ("the Dorothea in her") craved. Deronda's search for a "higher life" and the enthusiasm with which he embraced his duty resembled the effects of alcohol, and, as with alcohol, the result was confusion. That higher life, moreover, was denied to Gwendolen, for there was no equivalent of Zionism for her. Since she could not be redeemed by an inherited religion or race, everything that flowed from these ideas was "impotently wordy."[38]

Having briefly but decisively dismissed the bad half of the book, Leavis went on to a lengthy analysis of the good half. Here character, setting, dialogue, and language (all demonstrated by copious quotations) established the Gwendolen half—*Gwendolen Harleth,* as he now entitled it—as not only Eliot's best work but also as a model for other novelists. Henry James, Leavis insisted, would not have written *The Portrait of a Lady* had he not read *Gwendolen Harleth.* "Isabel Archer is Gwendolen and Osmond is Grandcourt"; indeed, *The Portrait of a Lady* was a variation of *Gwendolen Harleth.* The original, however, was far the greater of the two, even Eliot's minor characters revealing a "complexity and completeness" unrivalled by James, while her major ones were rendered "with extraordinary vividness and economy," "moral and psychological insight," and "luminous intelligence."[39]

As for the bad part of *Daniel Deronda*, Leavis said, there was "nothing to do but cut it away." *Gwendolen Harleth* had to be extricated from it and published on its own. The character of Deronda could be retained, but confined to his role as lay-confessor to Gwendolen. The resulting novel would have some rough edges, but it would be self-sufficient and substantial. *Gwendolen Harleth* would thus emerge as Eliot's greatest work, establishing her superiority not only to James, but to others who had been invoked as her rivals—George Meredith, who, compared to her, was a "shallow exhibitionist," or Thomas Hardy, a "provincial manufacturer of gauche and heavy fictions." Leavis had to go outside of England to find a novelist with whom she could be properly compared. Eliot, he admitted, was not "as transcendently great" as Tolstoy, but she was great, and "great in the same way." *Gwendolen Harleth* revealed the same psychological profundity and intense moral understanding of human nature as *Anna Karenina*. Leavis could pay Eliot no higher tribute: *Gwendolen Harleth*, had "a Tolstoyan depth and reality."[40]

In his introduction to a new edition of *Daniel Deronda*, in 1961, Leavis again declared it the work of a great novelist, indeed, one of the greatest novelists, and her "greatness at its most Tolstoyan." He now made it the source not only of James's *The Portrait of a Lady*, but also (by way of the character of Klesmer) of James's *The Tragic Muse*, although here too Eliot was much the superior. "She knows her English world better than James knows any world." The "clinching touch" was her influence on D. H. Lawrence, who studied her closely and felt that they shared the same abiding concern: the relationship of the individual psyche to the changing society. But even here, introducing a new edition of *Daniel Deronda*, Leavis made it clear that it was not *Daniel Deronda* itself he was praising. The title was a misnomer, because the character of Deronda was deeply flawed—not flawed, however, as others, or as he himself, had supposed. James's complaint about the coldness of the Jewish part, was only partially right. That part, Leavis now found, was the product not only of the "high-powered intellectual" in Eliot, but also of a "very positively feminine" aspect in Deronda, who displayed an emotional intensity and exalted idealism that were anything but cold. This was why the Jewish part failed—not because of Eliot's cold, analytic intellect but because of a powerful emotion that used the intellect for its own purposes.[41]

Early in his introduction, Leavis retracted the suggestion he had made in *The Great Tradition,* that *Gwendolen Harleth* be printed separately. That "surgery," he now realized, would be less simple and satisfactory than he had thought. An admirer of Eliot would properly insist upon reading the entire novel, and would be right to do so.* As Leavis went on, however, contemplating the defects of *Daniel Deronda* and the superlative merits of *Gwendolen Harleth*, he was tempted once more to try to separate it from *Daniel Deronda*. A dozen

---

* His hesitation to recommend that "surgery" might be related to the fact that the introduction appeared earlier, in October 1960, in the American Jewish journal *Commentary*, under the title, "George Eliot's Zionist Novel." It would hardly be fitting, in that context, to eliminate the Jewish theme from that "Zionist" novel.

The idea of an expurgated *Daniel Deronda* dated back to its original publication, when some enthusiastic Jewish readers performed that "surgery" in reverse, publishing a Hebrew translation without the Gwendolen distraction. (A more complete Hebrew translation, still somewhat abridged, appeared in 1893.) In 1878, a sequel to *Daniel Deronda* entitled *Gwendolen* was published anonymously in America. It had Deronda returning alone from Palestine, after the death of his wife Mirah, to marry Gwendolen—thus fulfilling the desire of some of the critics of the book who thought Gwendolen was the natural and proper wife for Deronda.

years later, he succumbed to that temptation and, with the encouragement of a publisher, actually prepared a volume to be called *Gwendolen Harleth*. The reader's report was apparently unfavorable and the project was abandoned.[42] The title page Leavis proposed was:

GWENDOLEN HARLETH
George Eliot's superb last novel
liberated from
DANIEL DERONDA

Leavis's first essay on *Daniel Deronda* in 1945 had a poignancy he may not have intended. The "Jewish question" had come into the forefront of the public consciousness with the gruesome revelations of the Nazi "solution" to that question. Even more fortuitous was the publication of *The Great Tradition* in 1948, the very year the state of Israel was founded. Leavis himself had no problem with Judaism or Zionism. If the Jewish part belonged to the bad half of the book, it was because of its artificial intrusion into the novel, a self-indulgence on the part of a noble nature.[43] Later, in his introduction to the new edition of the novel, he again praised the "disinterested and clear-sighted humanity" Eliot brought to the cause, a "nobility . . . tainted with self-indulgence."[44] His objections to the Jewish and Zionist themes were entirely literary and esthetic, not at all political or ideological.

This was not, however, as others have seen it. For good or bad, the book has taken on a political tone and judged as a Zionist manifesto. In his speech celebrating Israel's independence, Abba Eban, Israel's first ambassador to the United

Nations, extolled Eliot as "one of our first visionaries."[45] He might have quoted Theodor Herzl, who, more than half-a-century earlier, had credited *Daniel Deronda* with helping inspire his call for a Jewish state.* Fifteen years before that, there was the Lithuanian Jew Ben-Jehuda (née Eliezer Perelman), who dreamed of restoring Hebrew as the vernacular language of the Jewish people and was moved by a Russian translation of the novel to go to Israel to promote that cause. By the time the state was established, Israeli's three largest cities, Jerusalem, Tel Aviv, and Haifa, had streets named after George Eliot.

If *Daniel Deronda* has been praised by some for its prescient invocation of Zionism, it has been criticized by others for the same reasons. Zionism has become the culprit and Eliot the naive purveyor of a dangerous doctrine. In 1947, a reviewer in the *Times Literary Supplement* rebuked Eliot for apparently not having heard of Arabs, not knowing that they outnumbered Jews in Palestine, and not realizing that the Jews were the intruders in an Arab land.[47] A biography the following year made similar charges. Like many other critics, Joan Bennett preferred the Gwendolen part of *Daniel Deronda* to the Deronda part, but she went beyond that to criticize Eliot for ignoring the just claims of the Arabs, failing to foresee the international problems Zionism would bring in its wake, and making the novel a tool for Zionist propaganda.[48]

---

* An Israeli historian has cast doubt on this celebrated claim made by Herzl in *Der Judenstaat*. Herzl's diaries make it clear that he formulated his ideas about Zionism well before he heard of Eliot or *Daniel Deronda*. In 1895, just before the publication of *Der Judenstaat*, he wrote, "I must read *Daniel Deronda*. Perhaps it contains ideas similar to mine." Several months later, visiting London, he noted that the Chief Rabbi had pointed out to him that his plan was exactly "the idea of *Daniel Deronda*."[46]

More recently the anti-Zionist argument has taken a "post-colonialist" turn. Initiated by Edward Said in 1978 with the publication of *Orientalism,* the theory was applied specifically to *Daniel Deronda* the following year in *The Question of Palestine.* Eliot's novel, Said charged, typified the West's assumption of superiority over the East, and, worse, the refusal to attribute any reality to the inhabitants of the East. Mordecai professed to speak of the "Peoples of the East and the West," but the "felt reality" underlying that speech was only for the "Peoples of the West." Eliot revealed her complete indifference to the actual residents of Palestine by her silence on that subject, indeed, her "total absence of any thought." Contrasting a degraded East to a noble, enlightened West, she exemplified the "culture of high liberal-capitalism," the "ethnocentric rationale" that was at the heart of the "imperialist hegemony."[49]

Other critics have followed Said, not only in interpreting *Daniel Deronda* as a prime example of colonialism, but also by implicating Eliot personally in the imperialist enterprise. They cite the fact that her two stepsons chose to live and work in South Africa, and that she herself owned shares in South African and Indian railway companies. A considerable post-colonialist literature has echoed these themes.[50] The biography by Barbara Hardy in 2006 is more temperate than most, approving of Eliot's criticism of racism and anti-Semitism and her implicit disavowal of "Anglocentricity" revealed in her occasional expressions of internationalism and negative images of English society. But Deronda's Zionism is "unpalatable to the modern mind," for "we know the terrible past and present of Zionism, Palestine and Israel." Moreover, Eliot herself was "complicit" with the "gambling capitalists" who were responsible for Gwendolen's family's bankruptcy, because her own stock-market shares were an investment in the Empire and therefore unethical.[51]

When Eliot suspected, over a century ago, that the Jewish element would meet "resistance, and even repulsion," she never imagined (nor would even her sharpest critics have imagined) that it would meet quite this kind of resistance and repulsion. Yet it was almost as if she was anticipating the charge of "orientalism"—denying the reality of non-Jewish peoples in the East and assuming the superiority of the West—when she wrote in that moving letter to Harriet Beecher Stowe: "Moreover, not only towards the Jews, but towards all Oriental peoples with whom we English come in contact, a spirit of arrogance and contemptuous dictatorialness is observable which has become a national disgrace to us."[52] To a determined orientalist, of course, such a rebuttal in advance, as it were, only feeds the suspicion that there was cause for rebuttal.

Daniel Deronda has been spared some of the literary fashions of recent times—Marxism and deconstructionism, most notably—but not others: feminism (which has a rich lode of material in Gwendolen and Deronda's mother) as well as post-colonialism.[53] It may be taken as a tribute to the book that it remains a challenge to critics, as it is also an inspiration to readers.

EPILOGUE

Henry James concluded his review of Cross's biography of Eliot—a review that was not uncritical either of the biographer or of the subject—with a commendation of Eliot that transcended all criticism.

> What is remarkable, extraordinary—and the process remains inscrutable and mysterious—is that this quiet, anxious, sedentary, serious, invalidical [sic] English lady, without animal spirits, without adventures, without extravagance, assumption, or bravado, should have made us believe that nothing in the world was alien to her; should have produced such rich, deep, masterly pictures of the multifold life of man.[1]

This tribute was all the more generous because Eliot's capacity to embrace the "multifold life of man," to find nothing in the world "alien" to her, lay precisely in that part of *Daniel Deronda,* the Jewish element, that was alien to James himself. But it was just this element that made *Daniel Deronda* so remarkable, even extraordinary. And the process by which Eliot came to write it was not nearly as inscrutable and mysterious as James found it. Yes, Eliot was a quiet, anxious, serious, sickly English lady. But she was not at all sedentary. She travelled widely, engaged in intellectual adventures that took her far from her native land and culture, and exhibited, in her work as in her life, vigorous spiritual and moral, if not animal, spirits. She also displayed a bravado of thought and will that emboldened her to write and think and do as she liked—in the case of *Daniel Deronda*, to write what she knew would "satisfy nobody," would even be received with "repulsion" and "repugnance."[2]

What Eliot wrote, and what offended others, was a novel that was also an apologia, in the best sense of that word—not an apology but an explanation and vindication. It was an apologia for a Judaism that was virtually unknown to non-Jews (and to many Jews as well), and for a Jewish state that seemed even more bizarre, to Jews as well as non-Jews. When Shaftesbury and other Evangelicals called for the restoration of the Jews in Palestine, they did so in fulfillment of the Christian prophecy, as the precondition for the Second Coming of Christ. When Eliot did so, first by way of Mordecai and Deronda and then in her own voice (in her last essay), it was in fulfillment of the Jewish prophecy, the return of the Jewish people to their homeland. And while the Evangelicals saw Palestine as a religious haven for Jews as individuals, Eliot conceived of it as a state, a polity, for Jews as a nation.

An apologia, however impassioned, requires a serious confrontation with a worthy antagonist. This was the function of those two dramatic episodes in the novel: the session of the Philosophers club and the meeting with Deronda's dying mother. It was at the club that Mordecai addressed the arguments of the "rational Jew" who wanted a Judaism purged of its superstitions and exclusiveness, and of the non-Jew who regarded Jews as stubborn and arrogant and Judaism itself as "superannuated" by the law of progress. And it was with his mother that Deronda experienced the full force of the woman's case against Judaism, which had led her not only to repudiate her religion but also to give up her son so that neither she nor he would be burdened by that oppressive faith. Deronda's response to his mother was firm but gentle; anything more would have been unseemly. His real counterargument was existential, so to speak, in the person of his beloved Mirah, who, although a talented singer, had no desire to carve out "a path of her own."

The audacity of *Daniel Deronda* can be appreciated by contrast to another novel that would have been an obvious and more acceptable alternative to it. Assuming that, for some "inscrutable and mysterious" reason, Eliot was intent upon writing about Jews, she could have written quite a different novel about a different Jewish question. This would have been the question of anti-Semitism—not the virulent anti-Semitism found on the Continent (in the Damascus Affair, for example, or the Russian pogroms), but the "polite" anti-Semitism reflected in the prejudices, stereotypes, and discrimination that Jews labored under in England. These were the social disabilities that remained after the "civic disabilities" had been remedied by the grant of citizenship. This alternative novel would have dramatized those disabilities, would have found its hero in a "rational" Jew like Gideon or Klesmer, and would have depicted a Judaism that was humanistic, cosmopolitan, and progressive, in keeping with the temper of the times. It could even have made room for an occasional maverick or enthusiast like Mordecai, who would be tolerated by his coreligionists, and even by Christians, as an innocent and harmless dreamer, perhaps a prophet out of his time. This Jewish question could then be solved by the assimilation of a liberal, enlightened Jewry into a liberal, enlightened England. Such a novel would surely have earned the plaudits of critics and assured Eliot's reputation as the premier novelist of her time.

But this was not the novel that Eliot, after strenuous preparation and reflection, chose to write, because this was not the Jewish question that interested her or the kind of Judaism she had come to admire. Her Jewish question was not the relation of Jews to the Gentile world, but the relation of Jews to themselves, to their own people and their own world, the beliefs and traditions that were their history and their legacy. This Jewish question was predicated upon a robust Judaism, the creed of a nation that could find its fulfillment only in a polity and a state. If Eliot was prescient, as is often said (by critics as well as admirers) in anticipating the rise of Zionism and the creation of the Jewish state, she was no less prescient in recognizing the kind of Judaism that was appropriate to that state—not a defensive, beleaguered Judaism but an affirmative, even an assertive one.

Today, more than half a century after the founding of Israel, *Daniel Deronda* may be more pertinent than ever—not so much for the prediction of the state but rather as a rebuttal to a common rationale for the state based upon the familiar idea of the Jewish question. That idea was memorably expressed by Jean-Paul Sartre in a book published just after the end of the war, *Réflexions sur la question juive*, translated as *Anti-Semite and Jew*. "It is not the Jewish character that provokes anti-Semitism," Sartre declared, "it is the anti-Semite who creates the Jew." His Jewish question was the question of anti-Semitism, and his "necessary and sufficient" solution to that question was a socialist revolution that would finally eliminate anti-Semitism.[3] That solution has long since been discredited, but the conception of the problem, and, more important, the image of the Jew implicit in it, have persisted.

In much of the literature on the creation of the state, Israel has been represented as the response to the Holocaust, the refuge of a people that had been the victims of anti-Semitism in its most grotesque form. What made the Holocaust even more horrendous was the fact that the most barbarous event of modern times came at a stage of civilization which assumed such barbarities to be obsolete, and in a country that seemed to be at the very pinnacle of that civilization, boasting some of the most eminent philosophers, scientists, and artists of the Western world. If the Holocaust could have happened then and there, it could happen again at any time and any where. From this perspective, Israel seemed to be the last outpost of civilization for a haunted and hunted people. As the Holocaust is seen as the immediate cause and ultimate rationale for the creation of the state of Israel, so it is also seen as the defining event in Jewish history. And so, too, anti-Semitism may be seen as the defining identity of the Jewish people—the Jew as the eternal victim.

Daniel Deronda, long predating both the Holocaust and the founding of Israel (and the pogroms and Dreyfus Affair that motivated the leaders of the Zionist movement), presents a very different view of Jewish history and the Jewish people. It reminds us that Israel is not merely a refuge for desperate people, that the history of Judaism is more than the bitter

149

annals of persecution and catastrophe, and that Jews are not only, certainly not essentially, victims, survivors, martyrs, or even an abused and disaffected minority. For Deronda (as for Eliot), the Jewish identity was not imposed upon them by others. It was not the anti-Semite who "creates the Jew." It was Judaism, the religion and the people, that created the Jew. And it was Judaism that created the Jewish state, the culmination of a proud and enduring faith that defined the Jewish "nation," uniting Jews even as they were, and as they remain, physically dispersed.

If *Daniel Deronda* may be read as a refutation of Sartre (and, even more, of Said), it may also be read as confirmation of the view of Judaism put forward more recently by the one-time Soviet dissident and now Israeli citizen, Natan Sharansky. There is no reason to think that Sharansky has ever read the novel or even knows of the author. Certainly his own background is very different from that of Deronda or of Eliot herself—which makes it all the more remarkable that, well over a century later, his passionately argued tract *Defending Identity* presents a vision of Judaism and of the Jewish state that is remarkably similar to theirs.

Born in 1948, Sharansky was, as he says, "a typical, assimilated Soviet Jew," knowing nothing of Jewish religion, history, culture, or Israel—indeed, knowing nothing of the Holocaust although he lived in the Ukraine, "among the killing fields of the Holocaust." The only Jewish thing he did know was the Soviet identity card defining him, for himself and for others, as a Jew. His epiphany—his identity crisis, we would now say—came in the Six Day War, when he discovered his roots in "a unique history and people that stretched back more than two thousand years," and found in the victory of Israel the fulfillment of the "ancient Exodus from bondage to freedom, . . . a unique message of community, liberty, and hope."[4]

This was the beginning of the spiritual and intellectual odyssey that took Sharansky from a prison cell in the Soviet Union to a commanding position in Israeli society. There were two dramatic moments, as he recalled it, in that odyssey. The first was the "wildly liberating experience" of applying for a visa to emigrate to Israel—a doubly liberating experience, because it engaged him in the struggle for freedom and democracy, and at the same time, the struggle to "recapture my Jewish identity."[5] (The request for a visa may have been spiritually liberating, but it resulted in his nine-year imprisonment in the Soviet Union.) The second came some years later, in a memorable telephone call to his long-separated wife (she had managed to leave for Israel on the very morrow of their wedding), when he assured her that these two missions were not incompatible, that the particularistic values of Jewish identity and a Jewish state were not, as so many thought, at odds with the universalist values of freedom and democracy. The two, he persuaded her, were integrally related, the universal requiring the particular for its realization. It was this double vision of democracy and identity—the subtitle of *Defending Identity* is *Its Indispensable Role in Protecting Democracy*—that sustained Sharansky during all those years in his prison cell and, after his release, inspired him as a citizen of Israel, a member of the Knesset, a cabinet minister, and now one of Israel's most prominent public intellectuals.

There are uncanny echoes of *Daniel Deronda* in *Defending Identity*, most obviously the discovery by Sharansky, as by Deronda, of his Jewish identity and the elation that discovery brought with it. More remarkable is Sharansky's experience of his Jewishness as "a gravitational pull on the human spirit, an interconnection of souls," of souls that "interact across time and space," recalling Mordecai's conviction that the "soul" of one of the medieval sages was "born again within me," and that his own "long-wandering soul" would be transmitted to Deronda who would fulfill his mission.[6] Above all, it is the overriding message of Sharansky that is so strikingly similar to Eliot's: the idea of Judaism as a communal faith finding its expression in a national identity—a nationality, moreover, as elevating for the individual as for the nation itself.

This is Natan Sharansky in 2008:

> One universal quality of identity is that it gives life meaning beyond life itself. . . . Whatever its form, identity offers a sense of life beyond the physical and material, beyond mere personal existence. It is this sense of a common world that stretches before and beyond the self, of belonging to something greater than the self, that gives strength not only to community but to the individual as well.[7]

This was George Eliot in 1879:

> Not only the nobleness of a nation depends on the presence of this national consciousness, but also the nobleness of each individual citizen. Our dignity and rectitude are proportioned to our sense of relationship with something

great, admirable, pregnant with high possibilities, worthy of sacrifice, a continual inspiration to self-repression and discipline by the presentation of aims larger and more attractive to our generous part than the securing of personal ease or prosperity.[8]

Eliot's genius was in advancing these ideas well before the emergence of a Zionist movement, let alone the state of Israel. Sharansky's wisdom is in expressing the same ideas at a time when they are being challenged not only by post-Zionists within Israel but by post-modernists, post-nationalists, and post-colonialists abroad—and not only, as Sharansky notes, by such obvious enemies of Israel as Edward Said, but by those who belittle or disparage the very idea of nationality: the historians Eric Hobsbawm with his concept of "invented" nations and Benedict Anderson with his "imagined communities," or the philosopher Jürgen Habermas who favors a federation that would transcend, almost nullify, the nation-state. In deeds and in words, Sharansky stands as a rebuke to these critics and as a moving (if unwitting) testimonial to Eliot.

Eliot's personal odyssey was, in a sense, more dramatic than Deronda's (or Sharansky's). She did not, to be sure, discover her true faith in Judaism; nor did she undertake a pilgrimage to Palestine; nor did she organize a movement for the restoration of the Jews à la Shaftesbury. But her vision of Judaism and a Jewish state was all the more remarkable precisely because it was disinterested, because, unlike Deronda (or Sharansky), she was not Jewish and had no personal stake in it. It was still more remarkable because she came to it from a large philosophical perspective and from an intimate knowledge of the most sophisticated critics of Judaism. She knew everything her opponents (and some of her friends) might say in refutation of her views, having once shared some of them. Her conversion, not to Judaism but to a respect for religion in general and Judaism in particular, was all the more notable because it involved a repudiation of some of the most powerful ideologies of her time: the belligerent irreligion and anti-Judaism of the Young Hegelians, the attenuated, syncretistic religion of the Positivists, and the secular humanism of enlightened, "advanced" liberals.

Eliot was the rare novelist who was also a genuine intellectual, whose most serious ideas found dramatic expression in her novels. For her critics, this, as much as the Jewish element, is the near-fatal flaw of *Daniel Deronda*. To complain that it is overly "analytic"—a euphemism for "intellectual"—is to have an impoverished view of the novel as a genre and of this novel in particular, where the play of ideas is as much a part of the drama as the characters and events. Eliot was a novelist of ideas, much as Tolstoy and Dostoyevsky were; Leavis was quite right to compare *Daniel Deronda* in this respect with *Anna Karenina*. It is the quality and potency—and the prescience—of those ideas that made the novel so provocative at the time, and that make it so provocative and engaging today.

Daniel Deronda is an enduring presence in the "Great Tradition" of the novel—and an enduring contribution as well to the age-old Jewish question. Many novels of ideas die as the ideas themselves wither away, becoming the transient fancies of earlier times and lesser minds. Eliot's vision of Judaism is as compelling today as it was more than a century ago, very much part of the perennial dialogue about Jewish identity and the Jewish question.

NOTES

Key to Notes

Daniel Deronda	George Eliot, *Daniel Deronda* (New York, 1961 [1st ed., 1876])
Letters	*The George Eliot Letters*, ed. Gordon S. Haight (New Haven, 1954–5, 1977–8)
Notebooks	*George Eliot's* Daniel Deronda *Notebooks*, ed. Jane Irwin (Cambridge, Eng., 1996)
Cross	J. W. Cross, *George Eliot's Life as Related in Her Letters and Journals* (Boston, n.d. [1st ed. 1885, rev. ed., 1886])
Haight	Gordon S. Haight, *George Eliot: A Biography* (Oxford, 1968)

Prologue

1. *Letters*, VI, 238 (Journal, Apr. 12, 1876).
2. See below, pp. 137–40.
3. *Letters*, VI, 290 (to Madame Bodichon, Oct. 2, 1876).
4. Cross, I, 313.

5. Herbert Spencer, *An Autobiography* (London, 1904), I, 395 (letter to Edward Lott, April 23, 1852).

6. Edmund Gosse, *Aspects and Impressions* (1922), repr. in *George Eliot: Critical Assessments*, ed. Stuart Hutchinson (Sussex, 1996), II, 83.

7. *Letters*, IV, 364 (to John Morley, May 14, 1867).

8. A. O. J. Cockshut's *The Unbelievers: English Agnostic Thought 1840–1890* (New York, 1966). The chapter on Eliot opens: "George Eliot was the one great artist produced in the galaxy of Victorian agnostic talent" (p. 44).

9. Lord Acton, "J. W. Cross's 'Life of George Eliot' (1885), in Acton, *Religion, Politics, and Morality*, ed. J. Rufus Fears (Indianapolis, 1988), pp. 463, 485, 468.

10. Friedrich Nietzsche, *Twilight of the Idols* (1888), in *The Portable Nietzsche*, trans. and ed. Walter Kaufmann (London, 1976), pp. 515–16.

11. R. H. Hutton [unsigned], *Spectator*, Sept. 9, 1876, in *George Eliot: The Critical Heritage*, ed. David Carroll (London, 1971), p. 366.

12. W. H. Mallock [unsigned], *Edinburgh Review*, Oct. 1879, ib., p. 453.

13. *Notebooks*, pp. 493–516.

14. See below, Postscript to chapter III, pp. 101–4.

15. *Daniel Deronda*, p. 388.

16. *Notebooks*, pp. 162–3. The notebooks contain translations of other passages from this book.

Chapter One

1. Voltaire, "Jews," in *Philosophical Dictionary* (1764), from *The Works of Voltaire, A Contemporary Version*, trans. and ed. William F. Fleming (New York, 1901). (Text on the Internet: eBooks@Adelaide).

2. Arthur Hertzberg, *The French Enlightenment and the Jews* (New York, 1968), p. 301. For Eliot's remark, see *Letters*, I, 246 (to John Sibree, Feb. 11, 1848).

3. For Eliot on Voltaire, see below, chapter II, p. 54. For a sympathetic view of Voltaire and other *philosophes*, see, for example, Peter Gay, *Voltaire's Politics: The Poet as Realist* (Princeton, 1959) and other works by Gay; and Philipp Blom, *Encyclopédie: The Triumph of Reason in an Unreasonable Age* (London, 2004). For Voltaire and Jews, see Hertzberg; Adam Sutcliffe, *Judaism and Enlightenment* (Cambridge, Eng., 2003); and Ronald Schechter, "The Jewish Question in Eighteenth-Century France," *Eighteenth-Century Studies*, Autumn 1998.

4. Blom, p. 253; Hertzberg, p. 310.

5. See: J. W. Cross, *George Eliot's Life as Related in Her Letters and Journals* (Boston, n.d. [1st ed. 1885, rev. ed., 1886]), I, 149 (to Sara Hennell, Feb. 9, 1849).

6. Montesquieu, *The Spirit of the Laws* (1748), trans. Thomas Nugent (New York, 1949, II, 54–6. See also I, 364–5 on notorious instances of torture by English kings.

7. Hertzberg, pp. 339–41, 359–60; Jacob Katz, *From Prejudice to Destruction: Anti-Semitism, 1700–1933* (Cambridge, Mass., 1980), p. 109.

8. David Vital, *A People Apart: The Jews in Europe, 1789–1939* (Oxford, 1999), pp. 200–3.

9. Ibid., p. 237.

10. Immanuel Kant, *Anthropology from a Pragmatic Point of View* (1798), trans. Mary Gregor (The Hague, 1974), p. 77.

11. Kant, *Religion Within the Limits of Reason Alone* (1793), trans. Theodore M. Greene and Hoyt H. Hudson (New York, 1960), p. 116.

12. Katz, p. 57 (quoting Fichte, in 1793).

13. Kant, *Religion Within the Limits of Reason*, p. 154 n.
14. *Hegel's Philosophy of Right* (1821), trans. T. M. Knox (Oxford,, 1967), p. 169 (#270). See also a passage on justice and the law: "A man counts as a man in virtue of his manhood alone, not because he is a Jew, Catholic, Protestant, German, Italian, etc." (p. 134 [#209]).
15. Ludwig Feuerbach, *Essence of Christianity* (1841), trans. George Eliot (New York, 1957), pp. 113–14.
16. Bruno Bauer, "The Jewish Problem" (1842), in *The Young Hegelians: An Anthology*, ed. Lawrence S. Stepelevich (Cambridge, Eng., 1983), p. 189. (This translation of the title is odd. The German title, *Die Judenfrage*, is customarily translated as "The Jewish Question."
17. Ibid.
18. Karl Marx, "On the Jewish Question" (1844), in *Writings of the Young Marx on Philosophy and Society*, ed. David Lloyd Easton (New York, 1967), pp. 243, 248.
19. Marx, "Theses on Feuerbach" (1845), in Marx and Engels, *Basic Writings on Politics and Philosophy*, ed. Lewis S. Feuer (New York, 1959), pp. 243, 245.
20. Shlomo Avineri, *The Making of Modern Zionism: The Intellectual Origins of the Jewish State* (New York, 1981), pp. 40–41; Isaiah Berlin, "The Life and Opinions of Moses Hess," in *Against the Current: Essays in the History of Ideas* (Princeton, 2001), p. 224.
21. Walter Laqueur, *A History of Zionism* (New York, 1972), p. 47.
22. Moses Hess, *Rome and Jerusalem* (1862), Letter 5 (text on the Internet).
23. Ibid., Note 9.
24. In his essay on Hess, Isaiah Berlin said that little notice of the book was taken at the time, except among "educated German

Jews" upon whom it "fell like a bombshell" (p. 231). But it was not much of a bombshell even in that circle. Berlin also suggested that Lewes had met Hess in Paris and that he may have been the inspiration for Deronda (p. 246) But there is no evidence that Lewes had met Hess or knew of his book. Nor was his book in Eliot's library. (See Laqueur, p. 46; Haight, p. 471n.)

25. *Encyclopaedia Judaica*, VIII, p. 434.
26. Vital, p. 177.
27. Edmund Burke, *Reflections on the Revolution in France* (1790) (New York, 1961), pp. 60–1, 67, 97–8.
28. David Hume, *The History of England from the Invasion of Julius Caesar to the Revolution in 1688* (1778) (4 vols., Philadelphia, 1828), I, 377.
29. Adam Smith, *Lectures on Jurisprudence* (1762), ed. R. L. Meek, D. D. Raphael, and P. G. Stein (Oxford, 1978), pp. 527–8.
30. George Spater, *William Cobbett: The Poor Man's Friend* (Cambridge, Eng., 1982), II, 441, 591, n.79. This sympathetic biography confines Cobbett's most egregious comments about Jews to footnotes.
31. James Anthony Froude, *Thomas Carlyle: A History of His Life in London, 1834–1881* (London, 1884), II, 448–9.
32. "Thomas Carlyle" (Oct. 27, 1855) in *Essays of George Eliot,* ed. Thomas Pinney (London, 1963), p. 214.
33. *The Works of Lord Macaulay* (London., 1898), VIII, 3–4.
34. Ibid., p. 17.
35. William Flavelle Monypenny and George Earle Buckle, *The Life of Benjamin Disraeli, Earl of Beaconsfield* (London, 1929), I, 884
36. Vital, pp. 179–80.

37. Adam Garfinkle, "On the Origin, Meaning, Use and Abuse of a Phrase," *Middle Eastern Studies*, Oct. 1991.

38. Arthur P. Stanley, *Life and Correspondence of Thomas Arnold* (New York, 1910), I, 333 (to Rev. Julius Hare, May 12, 1834); II, 39 (to W. W. Hull, April 27, 1836).

39. Matthew Arnold, *Culture and Anarchy*, ed. J. Dover Wilson (Cambridge, Eng., 1966 [published serially, 1867–8, 1st ed., 1869]), pp. 13–14.

40. *Letters*, IV, 395 (Nov. 7, 1867). In 1873, Eliot casually quoted Arnold's expression, "sweetness and light," in a letter to Mrs. Mark Pattison (V, 460) (Nov. 17, 1873).

41. Edwin Hodder, *The Life and Work of the Seventh Early of Shaftesbury* (London, 1886), II, 478. (Italics in original)

42. For a discussion of the dispute over the origin and meaning of this expression, see Adam Garfinkle, "On the Origin. . .''; and Diana Muir, "A Land Without a People for a People Without a Land," *Middle East Quarterly,* Spring 2008.

43. G. F. A. Best, *Shaftesbury* (London, 1964), p. 69 (Dec. 16, 1847).

44. Hodder, III, 240 (Dec. 22, 1868).

45. Robert Blake, *Disraeli's Grand Tour: Benjamin Disraeli and the Holy Land, 1830–31* (Oxford, 1982), pp. 131–2.

46. Joseph E. Katz, "Awakening in the Christian World in Support of a Jewish Restoration, 1830–1930" (text on the Internet). The allusion to Romania was to the attempts to persuade Romania, which was especially anti-Semitic, to agree to civil rights for its Jews.

47. Barbara Tuchman, *Bible and Sword: England and Palestine from the Bronze Age to Balfour* (New York, 1988), p. 221.

48. Robert Blake, *Disraeli* (London, 1966), pp. 5–6.

49. Monypenny and Buckle, I, 240 (Sept. 1, 1833).

50. Tuchman, p. 222.

51. Monypenny and Buckle, I, 864.

52. *Tancred, or the New Crusade* (1847) (London, Collected Works, Longmans, Green, [n.d.]), p.149.

53. *Coningsby, Or the New Generation* (1844) (same ed.), pp. 213, 220.

54. *Tancred*, p. 8.

55. Ibid., pp. 40–1

56. Ibid., p. 124; p. 166.

57. Ibid., p. 262.

58. Ibid., p. 196.

59. Sarah Bradford, *Disraeli* (New York, 1983), pp. 94, 113.

60. Benjamin Disraeli, *Letters*, ed. J. A. W. Gunn, John Matthews, Donald M. Schurman, and M. G. Wiebe (Toronto, 1982), II, 42n (quoting speech by O'Connell, May 2, 1835).

61. Lawrence and Elisabeth Hanson, *Necessary Evil: The Life of Jane Welsh Carlyle* (New York, 1952), p. 413 (quoting Carlyle's notebook, Feb. 28, 1852); Monypenny and Buckle, II, 698.

62. For Eliot's view of Disraeli, as novelist and politician, see below, pp. 53–4 and 115–17.

63. R. H. Horne defended Dickens against this charge in *A New Spirit of the Age* (New York, 1844), p. 18. See also Amy Cruse, *The Victorians and their Reading* (Boston, 1936), p. 152.

64. *The Girlhood of Queen Victoria: A Selection from Her Diaries, 1832–59*, ed. Harry Stone (Bloomington, Ind., 1968), I, 13 (March 30, 1850).

65. Charles Dickens, *Our Mutual Friend* (1865) (New York, 1960), pp. 278ff.

66. Shirley Robin Letwin, *The Gentleman in Trollope: Individuality and Moral Conduct* (Cambridge, Mass., 1982), p. 74.

67. Anthony Trollope, *The Way We Live Now* (1875) (Oxford, 1951), II, 92–3, 277, 263, 362.

Chapter Two

1. *Letters*, III, 174–5 (to Sara Hennell, Oct. 7, 1859).
2. Ibid., I, 128–9 (Feb. 28, 1842).
3. On *Tancred*, see above, ch. I, pp. 53–4.
4. *Letters*, I, 246–7 (to John Sibree, Feb. 11, 1848) (italics in original).
5. Frederick Karl, *George Eliot* (New York, 1995), p. 93.
6. Sarah Bradford, *Disraeli* (New York, 1983), p. 186. See also *Coningsby*, where a young woman is described as "quite as devoted to her religion as Monsieur Sidonia can be to his race" (p. 348 [Bk. VII, ch. I]).
7. *Letters*, I, 177 (to Mrs. Bray, June 18, 1844).
8. Ibid., I, 322 (to Mr. and Mrs. Bray, Dec. 4, 1849).
9. Ibid., II, 153 (to Sara Hennell, April 29, 1854).
10. Ludwig Feuerbach, *The Essence of Christianity* (1841), trans. by George Eliot (New York, 1957), p. 271.
11. Ibid., p. ix.
12. *Essays of George Eliot,* ed. Thomas Pinney (London, 1963), pp. 223–30.
13. Matthew Arnold, *Essays Literary and Critical* (London, 1907), p. 121. (The current spelling is Jehuda Halevi.)
14. Ibid., pp. 121–4.
15. Ruth R. Wisse, *Jews and Power* (New York, 2007), p. 100.
16. *Daniel Deronda,* ch. 34. Two other chapters (62 and 63) have epigraphs from Heine.
17. See above, p. 2.
18. *Letters*, II, 423–4 (Dickens to Eliot, Jan. 18, 1858).
19. "Janet's Repentance," *Scenes of Clerical Life* (1858) (Phila., n.d.), p. 342 (ch. X).
20. *Letters*, IV, 64–5 (Nov. 26, 1862).
21. Ibid., p. 472 (to Clifford Allbutt, Aug. 1868).
22. Cross, II, 42 (Journal, July 16, 1858).

23. Haight, p. 323 (Journal, March 1860).
24. *Letters*, IV, 298 (to Sara Hennell, Aug. 10, 1866).
25. *Romola* (1863) (London, 1996), pp. 552, 558.
26. Edward Alexander, "George Eliot's Rabbi," *Commentary*, July 1991, p. 29.
27. Haight, p. 470 (Oct. 2, 1867).
28. *Letters*, IV, 399 (to Madame Bodichon, Nov. 16, 1867).
29. Haight, p. 470 (Spring, 1869).
30. Alexander, p. 30.
31. F. W. H. Myers, *Essays: Modern* (London, 1883), pp. 268–9.
32. *Letters*, V, 314 (to John Blackwood, Oct. 4, 1872). Lewes had earlier mentioned this scene in his diary: "Miss Leigh (Byron's granddaughter), having lost 500 £, looking feverishly excited. Painful sight" (Ibid., Sept. 26, 1872). The identification of Miss Leigh was in doubt, Lewes describing her as Byron's granddaughter, Eliot as his grand-niece. One biographer has identified her as Geraldine Amelia Leigh, Byron's niece (Karl, p. 501).
33. Cross, III, 180 (to John Blackwood, Nov. 5, 1873).
34. *Daniel Deronda*, p. 288; *Notebooks*, p. 101. See also William Baker, *George Eliot and Judaism* (Salzburg, 1975), p. 119.
35. *Daniel Deronda*, pp. 358–9.
36. Ibid., p. 388. (See above, Prologue, p. 8).
37. Ibid., p. 284. Irwin, in *Notebooks* (p. 37 n. 2), locates this quotation and two of the following as extracts from Graetz.
38. Ibid., p. 374. In her notebook, but not in the novel, Eliot identified him as "one of the younger Tanaim," a sage in the Mishnah in the first or second century. (*Notebooks*, p. 31 n. 2).
39. Ibid., pp. 356, 406 (see *Notebooks*, pp. 171–2).
40. Ibid., p. 385 (see *Notebooks*, 32 n. 2).
41. Ibid., p. 269.

42. Ibid., p. 276; p. 553.
43. Ibid., pp. 273–4.
44. Ibid., p. 297.
45. The description of Klesmer appears in *Daniel Deronda*, p. 32. Haight (pp. 489–90) argues convincingly that Rubinstein, not Liszt as Acton claimed, was the model for Klesmer.
46. *Notebooks*, pp. 249–51.
47. Cross, III, 170 (Journal, May 22, 1873).
48. *Daniel Deronda*, p. 382.

Chapter 3

1. Haight, p. 472.
2. *Daniel Deronda*, p. 1.
3. Ibid., pp. 4, 7.
4. Ibid., p. 11.
5. Ibid., pp. 12–13
6. Ibid., p. 26.
7. Ibid., pp. 49–50, 58–9.
8. Ibid., pp. 96, 99–100.
9. Ibid., pp. 111–12.
10. Ibid., p. 230.
11. Ibid., p. 241.
12. Ibid., p. 449.
13. Ibid., p. 611.
14. Ibid., p. 143.
15. Ibid., p. 152.
16. Ibid., p. 270.
17. Ibid., p. 289.
18. Ibid., p. 288.
19. Ibid., p. 355.
20. Ibid., pp. 373–4.

21. Ibid., p. 375.
22. Ibid., p. 376.
23. Ibid., pp. 377–8.
24. Ibid., pp. 385–91.
25. Rosemary Ashton, *G. H. Lewes: A Life* (Oxford, 1991), pp. 15–16; Gordon S. Haight, *George Eliot: A Biography* (Oxford, 1968), p. 489.
26. *Daniel Deronda*, pp. 394–6.
27. Ibid., pp. 397, 399.
28. Ibid., pp. 399–402.
29. Ibid., pp. 404–6.
30. Ibid., pp. 470–1.
31. Ibid., pp. 470–2.
32. Ibid., p. 471.
33. Ibid., p. 473.
34. Ibid., pp. 474–5.
35. Ibid., pp. 563–4.
36. Ibid., p. 477.
37. Ibid., pp. 477–8.
38. Ib., p. 481.
39. Ib., pp. 479.
40. Ib., pp. 498–500.
41. Ib., 501.
42. Ib., pp. 544–6.
43. Quoted by Paula Marantz Cohen, "Israel and *Daniel Deronda*," *Hudson Review*, Summer, 2002.
44. *Daniel Deronda*, p. 606.
45. Ib., p. 297.
46. *Notebooks*, pp. 81, 120–1, 123, 386, 408. On two occasions (pp. 120, 408), Eliot spelled the name as "Esra."
47. See below, chapter IV, p. 111.

48. *Daniel Deronda*, p. 288.

49. Ibid., p. 545.

50. Ibid., p. 544.

51. *Notebooks*, p. 181. For another reference to Kalonymos in the *Notebooks*, see p. 303. See also William Baker, *George Eliot and Judaism* (Salzburg, 1975) and Saleel Nurbhai and K. M. Newton, *George Eliot, Judaism and the Novels: Jewish Myth and Mysticism* (London, 2002).

52. *Letters*, VI, 242 (to John Blackwood, April 1876).

Chapter 4

1. *Letters*, VII, 78 (Nov. 21, 1878) (italics in original).

2. Ibid., p. 126 (April 5, 1879).

3. *Daniel Deronda*, p. 284.

4. George Eliot, *Impressions of Theophrastus Such* (1879), ed. Nancy Henry (Iowa City, 1994), pp. 146–8.

5. Ibid., pp. 148–52

6. Ibid., pp. 151–3.

7. Ibid., pp. 155–6.

8. Ibid., pp. 156–7.

9. Ibid., pp. 157–60.

10. Ibid., pp. 162–3.

11. Ibid., pp. 164–5.

12. Ibid., p. 164.

13. There are only a few passing references to Strauss and Feuerbach in letters in the early 1860s, and again in 1872 when she thanked the translator of Strauss's essays who had sent her a copy of his book (*Letters*, IV, 123, 139, 208; V, 282, 287; and VI, 110).

14. See above, chapter III, ftn. p. 88n.

15. *Daniel Deronda*, p. 403.

16. Benedict Spinoza, *Tractatus Theologico-Politicus* (1670), in *The Political Works*, ed. A. G. Wernham (Oxford, 1958), p. 63.

17. Michael A Rosenthal, "Spinoza the Crisis of Liberalism in Weimar Germany," *Hebraic Political Studies*, Winter 2008, p. 110. See also Milton Himmelfarb, *Jews and Gentiles*, ed. Gertrude Himmelfarb (New York, 2007), p. 24.

18. Bernard Semmel, in *George Eliot and the Politics of National Inheritance* (Oxford, 1994), makes a compelling case for nationality as a conservative principle underlying much of Eliot's thought and writing.

19. *Letters*, I, 193 (May 25, 1845).

20. Ibid., I, 246 (to John Sibree, Feb. 11, 1848).

21. Quoted by Thomas Pinney, ed., *Essays of George Eliot* (London, 1963), p. 415.

22. *Letters*, IV, 246 (April 26, 1866).

23. *Essays of George Eliot*, p. 422 (*Blackwood's*, January 1868).

24. See Gertrude Himmelfarb, "Politics and Ideology: The Reform Act of 1867," in *Victorian Minds* (New York, 1968).

25. *Letters*, V, 387 (to John Blackwood, March 14, 1873).

26. Ibid., VI, 21–2 (to Blackwood, Feb. 20, 1874).

27. Ibid., VII, 32 (to Blackwood, June 27, 1878); p. 47 (to François d'Albert-Durade, Aug. 1, 1878).

28. Ibid., IX, 282 (Edith Simcox's Autobiography, Dec. 26, 1879).

29. See Gertrude Himmelfarb, *The De-Moralization of Society: From Victorian Virtues to Modern Values* (New York, 1994), pp. 98–100.

30. *Letters*, IV, 364 (to John Morley, May 14, 1867).

31. *Theophrastus*, pp. 23–6.

32. See above, p. 77.

33. *Daniel Deronda*, p. 271.

34. Ib., p. 598.

Chapter 5

1. *Letters*, VI, 223 (Feb. 25, 1876).

2. Robert Blake, *Disraeli* (New York, 1966), p. 191.

3. *Letters*, VI, 227 (Mar. 2, 1876).

4. Ibid., p. 238 (Journal, April 12, 1876).

5. Ibid., p. 247 (May 9, 1876).

6. Ibid., p. 305 (Nov. 5, 1876).

7. Ibid., pp. 301–2 (Oct. 29, 1876).

8. Ibid., p. 275 (to John Blackwood, Sept. 2, 1876).

9. Letter of Freud to his wife, Aug. 26, 1882, quoted in Ernest Jones, *The Life and Work of Sigmund Freud* (New York, 1953), I, 174.

10. *Letters*, VI, 336 (Lewes to Edward Dowden, Feb. 1877).

11. Ibid., p. 379 (to David Kaufmann, May 31, 1877).

12. *Jewish Chronicle*, Dec. 15, 1876, in *George Eliot: Critical Assessments*, ed. Stuart Hutchinson (Sussex, Eng., 1996), I, 409.

13. R. E. Francillon, *Gentleman's Magazine,* Oct. 1876, in *George Eliot: The Critical Heritage*, ed. David Carroll (London, 1971) pp. 384, 395.

14. James Picciotto, *Gentleman's Magazine*, Nov. 1876, ibid., pp. 399–414. On the Lewes article, see above, p. 88n.

15. *Letters*, VI, 290 (to Mme. Bodichon, Oct. 2, 1876).

16. A.V. Dicey, *Nation*, Oct. 19, 1876, in *Critical Heritage*, p. 399.

17. *Academy*, Sept. 9, 1876, ibid., pp. 371–6.

18. *Saturday Review*, Sept. 16, 1876, ibid., pp. 377–8.

19. Edward Dowden, *Contemporary Review*, Feb. 1877, ibid., pp 446–7.

20. R. H. Hutton [unsigned], *Spectator*, Sept. 9, 1876, ibid., pp. 366, 370.

21. Haight, p. 417 (quoting James, May 10, 1869).

22. Henry James, "Daniel Deronda: A Conversation," *The Nation*, December 1876, appendix in F. R. Leavis, *The Great Tradition: George Eliot, Henry James, Joseph Conrad* (New York, 1948), pp. 249–66.

23. *Daniel Deronda*, pp. 32, 179, 304.

24. *Letters of Lord Acton to Mary Gladstone*, ed. Herbert Paul (New York, 1904), p. 155 (Dec. 27, 1880).

25. Lord Acton, "J. W. Cross's 'Life of George Eliot'," *Nineteenth Century*, March 1885, in Acton, *Religion, Politics, and Morality*, ed. J. Rufus Fears (Indianapolis, 1988), pp. 463, 472, 482.

26. *Cornhill Magazine*, Feb. 1881, in *Critical Assessments*, I, 628.

27. Leslie Stephen, *George Eliot* (London, 1902), pp. 187–200.

28. Bernard Semmel, *George Eliot and the Politics of National Inheritance* (Oxford, 1994), p. 117; Rosemary Ashton, *George Eliot: A Life* (London, 1996), p. 355.

29. Virginia Woolf, "George Eliot," *Times Literary Supplement*, Nov. 20, 1919, in Woolf, *Collected Essays* (New York, 1967), I, 201–4.

30. George Saintsbury, *Corrected Impressions: Essays on Victorian Writers* (1895), in *Critical Assessments*, I, 678.

31. G. K. Chesterton, *The Victorian Age in Literature* (1914), ibid., II, 73.

32. Edmund Gosse, *Aspects and Impressions* (London, 1922), ibid., p. 91.

33. David Cecil, *Early Victorian Novelists: Essays in Revaluation* (New York, 1935), in *A Century of George Eliot Criticism*, ed. Gordon S. Haight (Boston, 1965), pp. 199, 206, 210.

34. Lionel Trilling, "The Changing Myth of the Jews," in *Speaking of Literature and Society* (New York, 1980), pp. 73–6.

35. Trilling, "Little Dorrit" (1953), in *The Opposing Self* (New York, 1978 [1st ed., 1955], p. 46.

36. Trilling, "Dr. Leavis and the Moral Tradition" (1949) in *A Gathering of Fugitives* (New York, 1956); "The Leavis-Snow Contoroversy" (1962) in *Beyond Culture* (New York, 1965).

37. Claudia L. Johnson, "F.R. Leavis: The 'Great Tradition' of the English Novel and the Jewish Part," *Nineteenth-Century Literature*, Sept. 2001.

38. Leavis, *The Great Tradition*, pp. 80–5.

39. Ibid., pp. 85–6, 91, 99, 112–14, 123.

40. Ibid., pp., 122–5.

41. *Daniel Deronda*, pp. xiii–xxiii.

42. Leavis's preface, written in 1974, was published posthumously in the *London Review of Books* in 1982 and in a volume of his essays that year, *The Critic as Anti-Philosopher: Essays and Papers*, ed. G. Singh.

43. See above, p. 136.

44. *Daniel Deronda*, p. xvi.

45. Paula Marantz Cohen, "Israel and *Daniel Deronda*," *Hudson Review*, Summer 2002.

46. Shlomo Avineri, "Theodor Herzl's Diaries as a Bildungsroman," *Jewish Social Studies*, Spring/Summer 1999.

47. Johnson, p. 207 (quoting *Times Literary Supplement*, Aug. 2, 1947).

48. Joan Bennett, *George Eliot: Her Mind and Her Art* (Cambridge, Eng., 1948), pp. 186–7.

49. Edward W. Said, *The Question of Palestine* (New York, 1992 [1st ed., 1979], pp. 63–6.

50. See, for example, Susan Meyer, *Imperialism at Home: Race and Victorian Women's Fiction* (London, 1996), and Aamir R. Mufti, *Enlightenment in the Colony: The Jewish Question and the Crisis of Postcolonial Culture* (Princeton, 2007).

For other examples of this view, as well as an analysis and critique of it, see Nancy Henry, *George Eliot and the British Empire* (Cambridge, Eng., 2002). A detailed criticism of Said's interpretation of *Daniel Deronda* is Kenneth M. Newton's "Second Sight: Is Edward Said Right about Daniel Deronda?" *Times Literary Supplement*, May 9, 2008.

51. Barbara Hardy, *George Eliot: A Critic's Biography* (London, 2006), pp. 62–6.

52. See above, p. 122–3.

53. Feminist critiques have been directed more against *Middlemarch* than *Daniel Deronda*. See, for example, the essays in *Critical Associations*, pp. 115–234.

Epilogue

1. *Atlantic Monthly*, May 1885, in *Critical Heritage*, p. 504.

2. See above, pp. 122–3.

3. Jean-Paul Sartre, *Anti-Semite and Jew*, trans. George J. Becker (New York, 1948), pp. 143, 150.

4. Natan Sharansky, *Defending Identity: Its Indispensable Role in Protecting Democracy* (New York, 2008), pp. 11–13.

5. Ibid., p. 14.

6. Ibid., p. 33; *Daniel Deronda*, pp. 375, 406. (See above, ch. 3, pp. 85–6.)

7. Sharansky, p. 5.

8. *Impressions of Theophrastus Such*, pp. 147–8.

INDEX